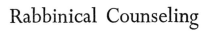

Rabbinical Counseling

Edited by
Earl A. Grollman

Rabbinical
Counseling

Contributing Authors

IRWIN M. BLANK · ISRAEL J. GERBER
ALBERT I. GORDON · EARL A. GROLLMAN
ROBERT L. KATZ · RICHARD L. RUBENSTEIN

BLOCH PUBLISHING COMPANY
New York

Contents

IRWIN M. BLANK, M.H.L., Ed.D.

Rabbi, Temple Sinai, Tenafly, N. J.; Ordination, Hebrew Union College (1950); Lecturer, Columbia University, Teachers College; Member of the faculty, Hebrew Union College School of Education.

ISRAEL J. GERBER, M.S., Ph.D.

Rabbi, Temple Beth-El, Charlotte, N. C.; Ordination, Jewish Institute of Religion (1941); Professor, Livingstone College; Author, *Psychology of the Suffering Mind* (Jonathan David), *Man on a Pendulum* (American Press), *Immortal Rebels* (Jonathan David).

ALBERT I. GORDON, M.A., M.H.L., Ph.D., D.D.

Rabbi, Temple Emanuel, Newton, Mass.; Ordination, Jewish Theological Seminary (1950); Past President, Massachusetts Board of Rabbis; former Executive Director, United Synagogues of America; Lecturer, Boston University, Andover-Newton Theological School; Author, *Jews in Transition* (University of Minnesota Press), *Jews in Suburbia* (Beacon Press), *Intermarriage* (Beacon Press).

EARL A. GROLLMAN, M.H.L., D.D.

Rabbi, Beth El Temple Center, Belmont, Mass.; Ordination, Hebrew Union College (1950); Past President, Massachusetts Board of Rabbis; Author, *Judaism in Sigmund Freud's World* (Bloch; Appleton-Century), *Into Pain, Through Pain, Past Pain—Teaching Death to Children* (Beacon Press).

ROBERT L. KATZ, M.H.L., S.T.M., Ph.D.

Professor, Human Relations, Hebrew Union College—Jewish Institute of Religion; Ordination, Hebrew Union College (1943); Lecturer, University of Cincinnati, Antioch College; Author, *Empathy* (Free Press).

RICHARD L. RUBENSTEIN, M.H.L., S.T.M., Ph.D.

Director, B'nai B'rith Hillel Foundation, University of Pittsburgh, Carnegie Institute of Technology; Ordination, Jewish Theological Seminary (1952); Charles E. Merrill Lecturer in Humanities, The University of Pittsburgh; Author, *After Auschwitz* (Bobbs, Merrill); *Studies in Contemporary Jewish Theology.*

"Ointment and perfume rejoice the heart; so doth the sweetness of a man's friend by hearty counsel."

Proverbs 27:9

Introduction

THIS is not a "do it yourself" volume offering exacting procedures and precise processes. There are no pat answers to life. Rather this book attempts to present the rich sources of our faith interlaced with the depth resources of social sciences. The rabbi as teacher and counselor must understand life before he can change life. Concrete, practical facts coupled with fundamental theory are vital to help people help themselves.

Rabbis who are experts in their field have given us the benefit of their specialized research and experience. The scope of their material goes beyond the compass of the oft-written issues of everyday life. There is already a proliferation of tomes concerning premarital counseling and ordinary grief reactions to death. Most sorely needed are organized, comprehensive approaches to some of life's problems which were previously uncommon but are now only too prevalent in the Jewish community. This book is designed to aid the rabbi, as well as to bring to the psychologist, teacher, and social worker a clearer understanding of Jewish attitudes on vital issues.

Sociologists, psychologists and historians have offered

varied reasons for the problems of intermarriage, divorce, juvenile delinquency, suicide, and the increased general loss of Jewish family values. The question is often asked: Can Jewish values enrich the mainstream without being swamped in the churning tides of the general milieu? A Chassidic rebbe once explained that there were two major tragedies which could befall the Jews. One was to be stripped of their liberty and forced to live in ghettos. When this happened in the past, the Torah flourished even as the spiritual values were cherished, yet the restrictions that were imposed were too great a burden to bear. The other tragedy, the rebbe asserted, would be for Jews to live free and unrestricted among their countrymen, but with the Torah forgotten and things of the spirit lost.

In the United States today, anti-Semitism is at an all time low and publicly out of fashion. Jews are experiencing an unprecedented freedom never known in ancient Israel or the golden age in Moslem Spain. There is freedom to adhere to the faith or abandon it; to emphasize differences or to become invisible. For the time being, the Jew has gained a sense of security in a new history without tears. He has progressed economically at an even more rapid pace than the country as a whole. In education, he is at a par with most culturally advanced segments of the American population. He is part of the Great Divide in American Jewish history, for he is the first generation to have achieved full acculturation in the acquired values of the United States. Unlike his immigrant parents or grandparents, he is American born, American educated, and an inherent part of the American middle-class. Since the end of World War II, the greatest change affecting the interactions of American Jewry with other Americans has been the rapid and far-reaching population shift from the cities to the suburbs. Two-thirds of American Jews live in suburban sections of standard metropolitan areas, often next door to Christian neighbors. For 2,000 years the Jews have learned to "sing the Lord's song" in bondage; now it remains to be seen whether they will learn how to sing His song in freedom.

Many have tried to eliminate and suppress those differences which distinguish them from other American groups. As the Jew strives to achieve "Americanization," he has a tendency and drive to be more "like" other Americans and less "unlike." When he was denied equality, he fought fiercely to be superior. Now that he is regarded as an equal, he tends to accept mediocrity posing as normalcy. Jewish group distinctiveness pales in proportion. The bonds between the Jew and his family life are loosed. The scales of values are leveled off. The assimilatory process aids in breaking down those social controls which were once inherent in the social pattern of this tightly knit and relatively isolated group. The sense of disintegration in Jewish life is related to the general crisis of values in American life. In the question of the rebbe: "How to achieve a distinctive religio-cultural identity that stresses Jewish family values and at the same time participate fully in an integrated and pluralist America?" Can the rivulet of Jewish distinctiveness maintain itself against the onrushing sea of mass American mores?

Whatever the reasons for the loss of Jewish family values, the rabbi must deal with the results of social disorganization. Counseling is a helpful approach for troubled people with social, emotional, and religious concerns. The aim is restoration of the person to wholeness—emotional, spiritual, and social. Self acceptance, acceptance of God, and acceptance of one's neighbor are all related goals.

Heretofore, rabbis were reluctant to enter the field of counseling. Many agreed with the psychiatrist, Dr. James Mann, who had cautioned the clergyman that since he lacked both knowledge and training, he should relegate the responsibility to trained professionals. Professor Seward Hiltner, a leader in the Protestant movement of pastoral counseling, lamented the fact that there are few Jewish books devoted to the scientific understanding of interpersonal relationships. He said the Jews apparently feel that where psychology is concerned, one should go to the professional psychiatrist; and this excludes rabbis since they are religionists.

On the other hand, psychological understanding of religion has been readily undertaken by sociologists, psychologists, historians, and Christian clergymen. J. G. Frazer, in his *Golden Bough* (1915), was one of the first to capture the public imagination by demonstrating the correlation between cultural anthropology and the dynamics of religion. At this time, Sigmund Freud was describing the psychoanalytical interpretations of religious emblems, practices, and beliefs. William James' *Varieties of Religious Experience* presented an empirical approach to the biographies of religious leaders. In America, G. Stanley Hall, George A. Coe, James H. Leuba, and Edward D. Starbuck were analyzing the psychology of religious phenomena.

Clinical training for a limited number of Protestant seminary students was launched in 1925 and became absorbed into the curriculum of the Episcopal Theological Seminary of Cambridge, Massachusetts. It was Dr. Richard Cabot who proposed a Clinical Year for Theological Students at an Atlantic Coast Inter-Seminary Conference in New York City. His argument was that the clergyman who graduated from a theological seminary should no more step out into full responsibility as pastor of a church than a medical school graduate should go directly into the private practice of medicine without having had at least a year to learn under supervision.

Anton Boisen was appointed chaplain at Worcester State Hospital in Massachusetts and inaugurated the plan of bringing theological students to the hospital for three months of work and study. Because of his own affliction with an acute mental disorder and because of his search for the meaning of that experience, he came to feel that the clergyman had much to learn from the study of the sufferings of the mentally ill and much to give in the way of understanding and support to these people who, up to that time, had been more or less neglected by the organized church.

Boisen was not so much concerned that his students be interested in therapy as he was that they develop understanding of the problems with which the patients were struggling. He did not want the students to provide a religious ministry for the patients. "I did not propose to bring in novices and turn them loose to do religious or therapeutic work," he said. In successive summer periods, Boisen continued to accept theological students for work and study.

Today, Christian clergymen like Wayne E. Oates, Paul E. Johnson, Edgar N. Jackson, Seward H. Hiltner, Reuel L. Howe, and Carroll A. Wise have done much to clarify fundamental relationships between theology and psychology and transvaluate this thought into a pastoral service for the congregation. The role of the churchmen in national mental health has been dramatically revealed by a report that 42% of emotionally troubled persons first seek a minister, and of these, 65% are satisfied with the help they received. Often the clergy is a more acceptable source of potential help than the social worker who still, unfortunately, carries the image to many as a "giver of charity," or the psychiatrist who may be viewed as a doctor who treats "crazy people."

In Judaism, relatively few rabbis have been seriously concerned with the counseling ministry. Many Jewish seminaries teach psychology and counseling, but in contrast to the Protestant theological schools, the courses are just footnotes. Jewish chaplains in hospitals and penal institutions are often not as well equipped and qualified as their Christian counterparts.

Yet, counseling has played an important role in the Jewish tradition. An indication of its significance is seen from a study of the Biblical words for "counsel." The Hebrew עֵצָה ("Etzah"), meaning "counsel" or "advice," is used as a substantive 84 times in the Bible. The verb יָעַץ ("Yaatz") connotates "to give or receive counsel" and "to advise." From this root is derived the Hebrew word for "counselor." These words signify "advice—given or received" and the "human or divine ability to form plans." *Isaiah* 11:2 describes the ideal ruler as one who demonstrates a quality of "the spirit of *counsel* and might."

A second interesting Hebrew word which is translated in English as counsel is the word סוֹד ("sodh"), meaning a "couch," "cushion," or "pillow." The phrase depicts "a consultation or counsel," or "an assembly—either of friends talking intimately, or of judges consulting together," or "the revealing of secrets." In *Proverbs* 15:22: "For want of counsel, purposes are frustrated: but in the multitude of counsellors they are established." סוד is also used to denote pleasant conversation and shared confidences as when the Psalmist (55:15) speaks of taking "sweet counsel together" with his close friends.

Throughout the centuries, the Jewish leader was compared to a *shepherd*. Scripture recalls Moses who likened himself to a shepherd, with Israel as the flock. One of his most plaintive cries to God upon relinquishing leadership was the solicitude over the appointment of a successor so "that the congregation of the Lord be not as sheep which have no shepherd." (*Numbers* 27:17) Just as God is the Shepherd of Israel so Israel's leaders must in turn care for His people.

The word *pastor* is the Latinized form of the Hebrew word for shepherd. The King James Version renders the Hebrew (shepherds), as *pastors* in *Jeremiah* 2:8. In the New Testament, *Ephesians* 4:11, the words *pastors* and *teachers* are joined together in depicting the twofold task of the ministry as both pastoral care and instruction. *Pascere* had the connotation of "pasturing" and "feeding." The pastor was to care for the spiritual interests of the people and feed their souls with spiritual food.

The Bible reveals various prototypes of the counselor. In the time of the patriarchs, disputes and problems were dealt with by the head of the family. Later, during the exodus and the wanderings, Moses became the outstanding judge. The people stood about him all day long. Jethro, Moses' father-in-law, believed this too heavy a burden for any one man. At Jethro's suggestion, Moses selected men who were experienced in handling problems in their own families and gave them the responsibility for small groups. (*Exodus* 18:13–26)

Samuel was the outstanding counselor during the era of the judges. Traveling extensively, he listened to controversies, rendered judgments, and reviewed adjudications.

The prophets were not counselors in the usual sense of

the word, but one cannot read Jeremiah and Ezekiel without sensing that here were men of God who were particularly interested in things of the heart. It is not difficult to feel that these great men would have lent a sympathetic ear to those who came to them with burdens. They realized that people have problems because they are people.

Of course, the great Jewish sages were not medical therapists in the contemporary sense. So in this book is the recognition that the functions of religion and psychology are different and cannot be indiscriminately interchanged. Psychiatry is not religion, nor is religion psychiatry. Psychiatry is a mental discipline carried on by a medically trained physician who has a license to practice medicine. Rabbis, too, are licensed but not for the same tasks.

The goal of the rabbi is not to engage in prolonged analysis of neurotic symptoms. His responsibility is to help the multitude. Support for emotional injuries is given in a healing relationship with others and with God. The rabbi is successful as counselor to the extent that he can offer such a relationship. This the rabbi can do as rabbi. Indeed, there is no more appropriate function for him who would point out evidence of the hand of God in the affairs of men.

Reports of the increasing incidence of profoundly painful encounters experienced by rabbis in their dealings with persons afflicted with great problems emphasize the need of rabbis for familiarity with clinical manifestations of mental illness and crisis situations. At the same time, the clergyman should not forsake his own traditional resources and functions in extending his loving concern, in sharing a religious orientation of life, a feeling of belonging, a power of faith, and a meaningful belief in God. He has his own unique framework of viewing and handling guilt, forgiveness, conflict, uncertainty, suffering, and hostility. His is a fellowship with a past, a present, and a future tied together by rites, theology, and a religious ethic. The practice of psychotherapy as the only real ministry to their congregation has led the Suffragan Bishop of Washington, Paul Moore, Jr., to write: "Too many priests forget their priestliness when

they learn some of the basic skills of counseling—or perhaps they have not been trained properly in the use of
priestly techniques and therefore are not confident in their
exercise. These clergy become 'clinical therapists' who happen to have the prefix 'Reverend' in front of their name."

A. A. Brill in his paper *Danger Signals for the Rabbi in
His Pastoral Ministry* mentions the mutual suspicions of
clergymen and psychologists. He emphasizes the need for
creative understanding. Especially does he remind the rabbi
of the basic teaching of Judaism: "Human actions should
not be ridiculed, bewailed nor detested, but they should be
understood." There is this similarity of concern: both rabbi
and psychiatrist are interested in man and the realm of family life. The psychiatrist can plumb the unconscious and
help overcome the fragmentation of the individual with
dynamic techniques and skills. The rabbi also can aid in
the formation of a vital and essential orientation to life with
a religious approach of sympathy, confession, and supportive
love. "True religion and true psychology," states the American Psychiatric Association, "are mutually enriching and
should have nothing to fear from one another." Often, the
conflict is not between science and theology, but between
individuals who are unable to understand one another.

Today, there are many types of counselors—vocational
counselors, educational counselors, marriage counselors,
health counselors, and rabbinical counselors. Even though
the fields are neither precisely coordinated nor accurately
defined, the disturbed individual often comes to that counselor presumed to possess special expertness. The rabbi is
ordained to meet the spiritual needs of his people. These
people have a claim upon him not only for compassion but
for aid. No trouble should seem too trifling or any sorrow
too insignificant to be worthy of his interest.

Despite the fact that he is not a medical therapist, the
rabbi may be of unique assistance. He represents a concerned religious community. His truest function is revealed
in terms of years, decades, as he watches children grow, mar-
ries them, and teaches their children in turn, and as he

stands beside loved ones around the death bed of a patriarch whom he has come to admire and respect. Beyond a crisis of faith people turn to him because of marital questions, parent-child problems, and a variety of inter- or intra-personal needs. He is minister, pastor, counselor to individuals and families in joy and adversity. He attempts to aid his people by giving them greater hope, understanding, and insight into their inner conflicts. At the same time, the rabbi is himself helped when he helps others in a dialogical interchange. The I and Thou relationship is according to Martin Buber "a religious experience" beyond the most knowledgeable theology and psychology.

In the parable of the Chassidic rebbe, Moshe Leib of Sasov: "How to love man is something I learned from a peasant. I was at an inn where peasants were drinking. For a long time all were silent until one person, moved by the wine, asked a man sitting beside him, 'Tell me, do you love me or don't you?' The other replied, 'I love you very much.' The intoxicated peasant spoke again, 'You say that you love me but you do not know what I need; if you really loved me, you would know.' The other had not a word to say to this and the peasant who put the question fell silent again. But I understand the peasant; for to know the needs of men and to help them bear the burden of their sorrow, that is the true love of man."

Earl A. Grollman, D. D.

I

Robert L. Katz

Counseling, Empathy, and the Rabbi

IN this survey we shall consider the nature of the rabbi's role as a counselor, his use of empathy as a resource in guidance, and some issues in the sociology of his role. How do we define the situation in which a rabbi meets a member of his congregation in a one-to-one relationship involving personal needs and not information or ritual? What does the rabbi have to contribute as a religious counselor? Since he is not exclusively identified as a counselor, what role conflicts does he face when he works with individuals outside the pulpit or the classroom?

The rabbi of the past functioned as the *dayan* or judge. He was consulted on matters of ritual and civil law which were to be interpreted in terms of an internally consistent and cohesive value system to which the total community subscribed. The rabbi derived his authority from his ordination as a teacher of the law and from his expert knowledge of the stipulations of the tradition. A somewhat closer analogy between the counseling activities of the modern rabbi can be found in the guidance of the Chassidic masters who were accepted as spiritual directors in quite personal matters. But viewed in the light of the main stream of Jewish tradition, the modern rabbinate represents a new and emergent role in the area of counseling. It incorporates psychological insights and extends into areas where the prescriptions of the traditional culture are either rejected or considered no longer relevant. Among liberal rabbis at least, decisions on ritual law are sought but infrequently and these are limited to specific phases of such life cycle experiences as marriage or bereavement. He rarely if ever functions as a judge in matters of civil law. The rabbi of the past who expounded the tradition to a community bound by its authority has been replaced by a less legally oriented religious leader who is now concerned more with attitudes and personal choices in the broader areas of ethics, belief, and family life. The rabbi's counseling grows organically out of his central function as a teacher, a preacher, and a priest rather than as a representative of a body of law.

Nearly all contemporary liberal rabbis are general practitioners rather than specialists. For them counseling is one of series of interrelated activities. They take a unitary role with multiple functions. This does not mean that rabbis carry the same orientation to every aspect of their work. As a counselor, the rabbi listens more than he speaks and empathizes more than he judges. But what he does as a counselor is compatible with the total role he fulfills both symbolically and actively.

What specific problems and situations do congregants bring to their rabbi? Many of the rabbi's encounters with individuals grow out of life cycle adjustments. Although the pre-marital interview is commonly a time for concluding priestly arrangements for the wedding ceremony, it is also an opportunity for the rabbi to help young people clarify their expectations of themselves and of the Jewish community. The rabbi's help is increasingly being sought by married couples who experience disillusionment and estrangement. They find themselves confused in their marital roles and often ask the rabbi to help them reconcile their differences. Parents turn to the rabbi for help with their anxieties over their children, concerned with problems of learning and of achievement. Teenage children and their parents turn to the rabbi for guidance in questions of sexual ethics and in problems related to vocational choices. The rabbi is viewed as a friend of the family, a confidante, and trusted adviser. People in middle age often bring up problems of religious faith. They want the rabbi's help in assessing their resources in facing the departure of their children, the problems of their retirement, their guilt in providing for the needs of their own aged parents. The aged themselves anticipate that the rabbi will show a personal and honest respect for them at a time when they feel rejected by their families and by the community. The rabbi is expected to visit the sick and counsel the bereaved. Responsibilities which were traditionally shared by the community are now specifically and insistently addressed to the rabbi as the most conspicuous symbol of the religious group.

Individuals also turn to the rabbi because he is the custodian of Jewish identity. However mixed their motives may be, the members of the congregation seek out the rabbi for help in problems of mixed marriage. They enlist his help as priest and as counselor, seeking judgment or justification in situations which for many American Jewish families constitute the sharpest expression of an identity crisis. The rabbi is often assigned the staggering task which tradition assigned to the prophet Elijah of turning the hearts of the children to the parents and the hearts of the parents to the children.

The rabbi's help is sought too by individuals experiencing psychological stress and emotional conflicts. Hesitant to consult a psychotherapist, individuals will turn to the rabbi for relief and reassurance. In such situations the rabbi's role is a kind of first aid. He offers acceptance and understanding and helps individuals overcome their fears of seeking intensive therapy.

Some questions brought to the rabbi deal with ethics. "Why should the Jew be involved in the civil rights movement?" "How can I live with my conscience and be an organization man?" Others deal with more existential questions. "Why should I survive as a Jew?" "What use is my life?" "Why does God allow so much suffering in the world?" "Why did this child have to die?" The rabbi preaches on such issues and deals with them in his adult education classes. They also arise in personal conversations not as academic questions but as acute and live options for which the rabbi's guidance is sought either directly or indirectly. The manner of putting the question varies. Sometimes the congregant approaches the rabbi defiantly and provocatively as if daring him to come up with an answer which the congregant is sure cannot be found. At other times the request grows out of a more dependent mood. "Since you speak of these matters from the pulpit, can you help me find the answers." The very accessibility of the rabbi, to say nothing of his symbolic role as a teacher of faith, lead individuals to consult him on existential concerns.

The range of needs is broad and the rabbi may expect that in the course of his career he will be consulted in almost every area of human experience. However rabbis may differ in their concern with counseling, they are increasingly perceived by laymen as resources in living. Some laymen want authoritative answers. Others want the rabbi to be no more than a companion to them in their search. For some he symbolizes charismatic power, for others the indulgence of a mother or the conscience of the father. Even in a secular environment, he is viewed as a representative of God. Those who profess no faith feel they are entitled to call on him for help in personal and ethical dilemmas. What is unique in the rabbi's role is his availability and accessibility. No other professional in human relations is the object of so many diverse expectations from such a variety of individuals.

The Context of Rabbinical Counseling

Counseling for the rabbi remains a somewhat ambiguous role. It is not formally structured or defined as is the case with other professionals. There are no commonly accepted procedures to guide the rabbi in his meetings with laymen.

Since counseling has not yet become institutionalized, the rabbi's activities in this area are almost coextensive with his other roles.

Professional counselors have carefully trained themselves to become aware of the subtleties and nuances of their personal meetings with clients. They have subjected their transactions to minute psychological and sociological analysis. They have also developed norms and professional attitudes which add to their effectiveness at the same time that they serve as techniques for maintaining a clear and consistent professional self-image. They have relatively sharp guidelines for defining professional relationships and for clarifying the character of interviews.

The situation is quite different for the rabbi who meets individuals in a great variety of contacts. Often the professional and the social elements merge so that the rabbi is not conscious of distinctions between the teaching and the counseling encounter or between casual social engagement and a more personal helping relationship. The ambiguity in the rabbi's counseling role arises from the fact that there is no consensus among rabbis or among rabbis and laymen regarding the standards and practices of the profession. Now that counseling is becoming a more familiar and integral part of the rabbi's role, we may expect him to develop greater sensitivity to the dimensions of counseling and to distinctions among the variety of encounters he has with laymen. His effectiveness as a counselor depends to a considerable degree on his ability to recognize a personal message for what it is and to recognize when his role as teacher, priest, or administrator takes on the aspect of counseling, with all the problems, challenges, and opportunities associated with it. Divergent messages are addressed to the rabbi and no little skill is needed to respond relevantly to the character of each.

A counseling orientation helps the rabbi codify some of these personal messages and to distinguish between what is intellectual and what is personal, between what is objective and what is existential. The rabbi achieves such a counseling orientation through experience and through careful self-examination. He develops a kind of inner radar by which he can identify what is emotionally charged and vested with private meaning. Such alertness to the emotional overtones of messages is not easily achieved. Often the rabbi may listen attentively to the communications of another person and find his attention limited to the manifest content of what is being said. He may miss the unverbalized theme of the dialogue and act as though only questions of fact were involved in the discussion. Other professionals who use fixed routines with office facilities and fixed appointments have the opportunity of getting set for their communications with others. The very structure of their situation keeps them alert and prepares them for the unexpected. In his own role, the rabbi often has no reinforcement for his activities as a counselor. He has not yet developed techniques for structuring the encounter. He is, after all, primarily a teacher, one who transmits information and shares his own emotional investment in Judaism with others. He is wrapped up with the content of his teaching. He is simply not accustomed to suspending his own leadership role and devoting his attention to the fuller meaning of what is being addressed to him as a counselor. Another orientation is needed, a readiness for a shift from the self to the other, a change from pronouncement to active listening. In the example that follows, the shift came too late.

A young woman is introduced to a rabbi in a social situation. Seated at lunch, they exchange amenities. The rabbi is friendly and interested. The young woman, a stranger in the community, enjoys a personal meeting with the rabbinical leader. As the conversation develops, she comments on a magazine article which dealt with the phenomenon of the "Vanishing Jew." She asks for the rabbi's reactions to this article. The rabbi responds by saying that the author is entirely too negative, that the future of the Jew is really quite secure and that there is no reason, in his judgment, to despair of a vital Jewish community life in this country. The young woman listens attentively to the rabbi, but obviously her curiosity is not put to rest. She knows a number of Jews who are indifferent to their faith and feels the rabbi does not fully appreciate the seriousness of the problem. At this point in the conversation, the rabbi was tempted to continue the debate. He had relevant facts and data. He had already preached a sermon in which he felt he had ably disposed of the arguments raised by the author of the article. Up to this point, he was responding intellectually to his conversation partner. Had he been more aware of the feelings attached to this subject by a young woman who was not a professional student of Jewish life, he might have anticipated the trend that the conversation was soon to take. The young woman began to speak about the rituals of Judaism, about the tendency of Jews to isolate themselves socially, about the lack of religious faith she observes among her fellow Jews, and the intensity and genuineness of religious conviction that she finds among her Catholic friends. What is happening in the conversation? The subject area has moved from the contents of a magazine article to the felt experiences of an individual. But the rabbi is still not aware of the transition. He knows that he can document his arguments, but he is dimly aware that the young woman is now speaking somewhat intensely of her personal responses as a Jewess. With virtually no encouragement from the rabbi, the young woman now proceeds to supply details of her own life situation. She is soon to be married to a young man with a strongly traditional orientation. She discusses her ambivalent feelings about the place of ritual. She wonders whether she will be capable of meeting her husband's expectations and she indicates that she is not at all sure that Jews ought to survive as a separate group. The problems she had originally raised regarding the article on the "Vanishing Jew" are now clearly related to her ambivalent feelings about her forthcoming marriage and her own uncertain identification with the Jewish community. It was relatively late in the discussion that the rabbi recognized that the core of the message being addressed to him grew out of a personal existential situation. He was not being asked to comment as an expert in Jewish sociology but to respond as a religious counselor.

An experience of this kind indicates the difference be-

tween the manifest and the latent content of a message. It is
not at all unusual for a rabbi to receive messages in which
there is a hidden agenda. Only if he is aware of the fact that
the questions put to him may have a strongly personal com-
ponent can he decide on the course to follow. He may choose
to discuss objective facts as a scholarly authority, permit the
more personal material to emerge and respond as a counselor
then and there, or suggest a subsequent meeting when the
issues can be explored in personal terms on an occasion
recognized both by rabbi and congregant as involving counseling rather than academic discussion. The caseworker or
psychotherapist is not likely to be as involved as the rabbi in
situations in which the individual is only indirectly or partly
aware of the fact that he is requesting help with a personal
problem. The help of professionals is sought by means of an
appointment and the agenda is clearly concerned with feelings of self. The rabbi, on the other hand, often receives dis-
guised requests for personal help. Even the congregant may
not be aware of the fact that the presence of the rabbi, even
in social and unstructured situations, signals a helping figure
who is accessible without distinction to those whom he meets.
The rabbi is seen as a public figure serving the community
rather than as a professional specialist who contracts for his
time with individual clients. To speak to the rabbi does not
call for a commitment to a counseling relationship or even a
direct acknowledgement that one is seeking personal help beyond what is available as a member of the congregation listening to a sermon or participating in a class discussion. On
the other hand, the very variety of contacts which the rabbi
confronts in his ministry provide him with rare opportunities
for human helpfulness. Without a counseling orientation he
is likely to miss many situations where genuine dialogue
might have been possible.

The Domains of Counseling and Psychotherapy

Rabbinical counseling has a validity of its own and need
not suffer by comparison with psychotherapy. Now that specialists in human relations are invested with authority and

endowed with prestige, the rabbi may feel himself to be no more than a superficial practitioner of the art of human relations. Such a self-image would be inappropriate and unjustified. The rabbi is not an amateur therapist; he simply fulfills a different and distinctive role. His unique effectiveness is diminished if he views himself as a competitor. There is no objective reason for the rabbi to deprecate his own responsibilities which differ in content and scope from those of the psychotherapist.

The rabbinical counselor does not do uncovering or evocative psychotherapy or attempt to offer interpretations of unconscious dynamics. His counseling, while psychologically sensitive, is more phenomenological than psychodynamic. Does this mean that what he does as a counselor is shallow or that he is condemned to the status of an amateur? He would open himself to the charge of dabbling in psychotherapy if he did undertake, without appropriate training, to treat individuals who have chronic emotional problems. While the rabbi may collaborate with psychiatrists in the care of a specific individual, it is rare that a rabbi attempts to take therapeutic responsibility for psychiatric patients. The rabbi's concern is with individuals whose problems fall within the range of normal difficulties in living. As he offers guidance to such individuals, he helps in a realistic and appropriate way. He is competent, qualified, and relevant when he offers guidance and clarification to individuals who do not require intensive psychotherapy.

It is an error to think that counseling is significant only when it deals with the unconscious. The rabbi who helps individuals to cope with the realities of everyday experiences and with problems connected with the search for ultimate meaning may actually be coping with what is truly fundamental and vital. Often the religious counselor deals with problems, moral, theological, and existential, in which the psychiatrist claims no competence and for which he has no professional qualification. The rabbi deals with ultimate questions which are different in kind from the highly specialized and exceedingly individualized concerns of psychotherapy. The stake in one case is a standard of normal mental health and life adjustment; in the other, it is a stake between an uninspired, defeatist existence and meaningful living. In a sense the rabbi takes on a task of the deepest dimensions. He is called upon for a kind of courage which dismayed even Freud himself who once wrote

> "Thus I have not the courage to rise up before my fellowmen as a prophet and I bow to their reproach that I can offer them no consolation: for at bottom this is what they are all demanding—the wildest revolutionaries no less passionately than the most virtuous believers."

The rabbi has enough responsible and serious work to do as a counselor and religious guide without having to extend his role by becoming a quasi-therapist. Religious counseling is, of course, greatly informed by the insights of psychotherapy. The rabbi borrows some interview procedures. He learns to become sensitive to danger signals. He appreciates the pull of dated emotions on the responses of individuals to current life situations. He learns also the part that his own emotional responses play in personal encounters. All this and more he has borrowed from the specialist but the uses to which he puts this expert knowledge are determined by the needs of his own situation and the problems of his congregants rather than the goals of the psychotherapist or the procedures of the clinic. There is no need for the rabbi to become confused about his own role as long as he sees himself as a guide and teacher who relates himself to the total personality of his partner in the dialogue. The rabbi is not primarily concerned with models of mental health; his concern is properly with counseling and guiding individuals seeking fuller and more meaningful personal lives.

Empathy and Rabbinical Counseling

Much as they differ in their goals, both the rabbinical counselor and the psychotherapist use empathy, a process of feeling in to the other person. We shall define it and describe its place in the rabbi-congregant relationship.

The process of counseling itself is difficult to describe because the words cannot capture the essence of the relationship between the counselor and the counselee. Procedures appear contrived, artificial, and manipulative, when they are abstracted from the real relationship of individuals. It is particularly difficult to express the nature of empathy, a process by which the counselor feels himself into the experience of the other person. For the rabbi the empathic relationship is one of the most significant and meaningful contributions he may make in serving his congregant. Real empathy engenders acceptance and understanding. It forms the basis of the actual dialogue.

To be sure the rabbi uses a number of procedures which add to his technical competence. They help create the conditions out of which an empathic encounter may arise. The rabbi who interviews a congregant attempts to create a climate of acceptance in which the congregant may feel free to ventilate his feelings, his hopes, and his confusions. By rephrasing, repeating, and indirect questioning, the rabbi assists the individual to put his feelings into words. By this means he helps the individual gain some sense of mastery over vague and unverbalized feelings which may now be judged and placed in perspective. The rabbi helps the individual confront himself and to become increasingly aware of the ways in which he structures his experience Often the rabbi becomes a mirror reflecting back to the congregant the needs and conflicts which he has been unable to recognize in himself. But the rabbi is not only the neutral and passive listener. He offers suggestions and alternatives which grow out of his hard won understanding of the situation of the other person. Because he has genuine respect for the integrity of the congregant's personality, he does not impose these suggestions upon him with the authority of his position: his manner is tentative and suggestive rather than authoritarian. Ideas are offered for consideration. The rabbi does not in any way indicate to the congregant that he has a personal stake in persuading him to accept them. He avoids manipulating the congregant and seeks rather to help him become freer to choose ways of feeling and reacting that will be less self-defeating. An empathic attitude on the part of the rabbi keeps him from using the techniques of counseling in a mechanical, controlling, and impersonal way. Without empathy there can be no real communication between individuals, no mastery of the distance which keeps one person from apprehending what the other actually experiences. To empathize is to feel with the other person, to see with his eyes, to hear with his ears, and to stand in his shoes. Empathy helps make the technique of counseling more effective but in itself it is more of an orientation or a response than it is a routine or a procedure that can be deliberately and systematically practiced at the will of the counselor.

The rabbi represents a religious tradition in which the empathic theme is strongly emphasized. When he counsels empathically he is expressing one of the major motifs in Judaism and translating into human relations here and now the religious value of real participation in the experience of others. The theological basis of empathy is *imitatio Dei*. God is the partner in the sorrows of His people. When man empathizes with his fellow-man, he emulates God whose métier is lovingkindness. *Psalm* 91.15 speaks of God being with man in his trouble. The prophet Isaiah portrays the servant of God as being afflicted in all afflictions of his people. God identifies with his people, i.e., he makes himself similar to them and becomes involved in the human situation. The tradition teaches that the divine spirit accompanies the people in their exile. The idea of empathy is also expressed in the statement of the rabbis concerning the prerequisite for proper judgment. "Do not judge your friend until you have come unto his place." Empathy is therefore more than intellectual assessment; it involves an experience on the part of the judge or the counselor calling on him to transpose himself into the position of the other person and live through a situation which is different from one's own. The empathic theme is especially strong in the teachings of the Chassidim. They spoke of the "descent" of the Tzaddik or religious master. The master goes down to the level of the people, enters the pit in which they are sunk, experiences their fate as they live it, and then rises with them. In order to keep from being lost in the pit with the sinner, the master binds a rope of faith around himself. He immerses himself in the situation of the other person but is capable of extricating himself. Psychologically speaking, the Tzaddik protects himself from over-identifying and maintains a link with his own separate identity. The modern rabbinic counselor who would practice sympathetic understanding implements one of the most profound and relevant religious values of Judaism. His challenge is to become as sensitive as possible to the situation of the other person. The mandates of Judaism reinforce him in his role as empathizer.

What contributions does empathy make to the counseling activity of the rabbi? First, it provides him with an understanding that is intimate, immediate, and direct. Second, it creates the conditions essential for a supporting relationship.

The religious counselor must be capable of empathizing because he cannot expect to understand his people without drawing on his own subjective involvement He cannot rely on words, labels, and classifications. He cannot be confident that simply identifying the problems of another person logically and conceptually gives him an understanding of that person as he really is. In counseling, the rabbi does not give up the rational process of defining and analyzing; he supplements it with the tools of understanding that are appropriate to the appreciation of inner experiences. Words and concepts are useful as far as they go but they do not go far enough. The rabbi requires an understanding that comes from within. He may achieve this by participating imaginatively in the experiences of the other person. What he seeks is concrete, specific knowledge of individuals, the private world in which they live, the specifically personal elements of their life situation.

The use of empathy is indicated because counseling deals with private and personal versions of what are universal emotions and common human predicaments. In the grief experience when children feel themselves abandoned, the sense of abandonment on the part of one child has a special and unique quality, remaining a private emotion even though experienced universally in some form. Our knowledge of grief provides us with a background from which we must move on to more personal understanding. We may know something of the problems faced by the woman in middle age who wishes to resume creative work. We would hope that empathy will enable us to appreciate what taking a position means at this particular moment to the individual. We know that an aging person may have a tendency to be depressed and to feel resentful of the children on whom he is dependent for financial support. We need to appreciate what the particular individual feels are his own justifiable expectations of love or why he may feel a need for self-punishment. We tend to seek analogies and to attempt to understand one phenomenon in terms of another. But emotions are private and there comes a time when we must abandon the analogy and consider each individual in terms of his uniqueness. Jewish tradition reminds us that while individuals share a common identity, each represents something *sui generis*. God created all men from a single mold, yet each individual stamped from the same mold has something that distinguishes him from others. Empathy helps the rabbi appreciate the distinctively individual in human experience. It is a method of knowing which is specially suited to the human material.

Even when we acknowledge the fact that empathy is possible in relationship with individuals, we must be prepared to realize that continuously fresh and original acts of empathy are necessary to understand the other person, his changing responses, his shifting frames of reference. Empathy consist of a series of temporary identifications. One never really knows when it will yield a fragment of understanding. One must be prepared for the fact that even a moment of quick and genuine understanding must soon be supplemented by additional acts of empathy. There is to be sure a cumulative degree of understanding, but the process of empathy is never static nor complete.

Even when his empathy is most immediate and direct, the rabbi must be prepared for a degree of frustration. He can never be as fully attuned as he would like to the experience of another person because personality is elusive, spontaneous, and dynamic. There are depths and nuances of feeling that transcend the reach of even the most sensitive counselor. Incomplete and limited as it may be, empathy still makes possible a depth of understanding which other more logical and verbal methods cannot yield. No more can be expected of the rabbi than a willingness to suspend his objective stance for the moment and enter as fully as he can into the private world of another person. The gains of such understanding will ultimately accrue to the congregant and be deeply appreciated by him.

Contrived or simulated empathy is quickly recognized by the layman. He knows intuitively whether or not the rabbi has entered into meaningful rapport with him. When he becomes conscious of the empathy that has been evoked in the encounter, the congregant has the rewarding feeling of being accepted, of being appreciated as a person and not as a problem or a case. He is gratified to realize that he now exists as a vital reality and a real presence in the feelings of the counselor. He feels less lonely and less frightened because he now knows that another person genuinely accepts him.

Closely related to the feeling of acceptance is the satisfaction of feeling understood. He gains the confidence that there is a chance that he too will understand himself now that his situation makes sense to another person. There is a sense of relief too in the recognition that he is able to share his burdens with another person. He feels restored to a community and his own feeling of humanness is reinforced.

There is an ever present risk in empathy both to the rabbi and the person he wishes to help. It is the danger of losing objectivity and of failing to balance empathy with detachment and analysis. Empathy in itself is not only not enough for full understanding; it can seriously distort and complicate human relationships unless it is used with self-control and unless it is alternated with rational judgment.

It is all too common for the rabbi to over-empathize and to over-identify. He may feel that he has a particular talent for empathy and that his religious tradition makes him unusually responsive to the needs of others. Who should be sympathetic, open, and generous if not the rabbi who speaks of God's mercy and lovingkindness? Actually he requires no less self-disipline than a secular counselor. A sympathetic orientation can yield an extravagant and undiscriminating emotionality that can be destructive. The rabbi seriously errs if he believes that he can make up for possible deficiencies in technical understanding by the warmth and intensity of his emotional involvement. He must be able to set limits to his identifications. He could not long persevere as a counselor if he lacked the ability to detach himself from his encounter with others. To function effectively he must be able to assess logically and critically what happens in the personal relationships he establishes.

Empathy involves letting go of one's controls, but only for a moment. One yields to a feeling of participation and communion. But at times it is necessary to interrupt an identification to avoid being drawn in the magnetic pull of another's emotions. Far from being a sign of the depth of one's care for others, over-identification may betray a lack of respect for the other person.

In every empathic meeting there is the danger that the rabbi may lose sight of the fact that he and the other person have independent lives and that the problems of the other person belong to him alone and must be worked through by him. The rabbi fails if he becomes so burdened with the problems of others that he cannot distinguish between his personal life and the experiences that objectively belong to the other person. While the rabbi must be able to immerse himself in the life situations of others, he must also retain the power of extricating himself. In an excess of empathy, he may lose control of his own feelings. He then ceases to be a strong figure with whom the congregant can identify and his usefulness comes to an abrupt end.

In successful empathy there must be a shuttling between

involvement and detachment. Detachment itself can be an act of real service to the congregant because he requires an appreciation of the fact that he is a unique person with a destiny of his own. From the standpoint of the rabbi, such a restoring of the distance between the congregant and himself is necessary for gaining a perspective on the total counseling process. He must be able to detach himself too in order to avoid the emotional drain of an unrelieved absorption in the problems of others. He must also be alert to the possibility that his own problems and confusions will be reawakened in deep empathic meetings. He must be able to interrupt the empathic process and sift out what anxieties are his and what anxieties belong to the congregant. Far from being a mere protective technique, detachment is important for an understanding of the problems of the congregant as they exist for him, apart from whatever analogies they may have in the rabbi's own experience. Seated beside a congregant who mourns the loss of a father, the rabbi may find that his own grief for a deceased parent has been reawakened. He is caught up in the emotional contagion so that private memories are stirred up and old feelings of guilt and anger make themselves felt once more. The well intentioned sympathy he offers at such a moment may actually be a feeling of self-concern. The reassurance he offers, however well intentioned consciously, may be something that he feels he really needs himself. The rabbi is capable of over-reacting to a loss which may not be felt quite so keenly by the congregant himself. The center of interest has subtly shifted to the rabbi himself. Respect for differences is also part of empathy and love. Pure empathy untempered by judgment is no more useful than cold objectivity untouched by involvement.

Role Stresses

The rabbi not only faces the hazards which confront all counselors but in addition to these confronts certain stresses deriving from his role as a religious leader. As a public figure he has vulnerabilities built into his role which can seriously limit his effectiveness in helping others. Both an awareness of the unique structure of his role and a degree of self-knowledge can serve to help the rabbi cope with these strains.

Like other counselors the rabbi faces the task of keeping confidences inviolate. The rabbi lives with facts and experiences gained from intimate knowledge of others that he cannot reveal in conversation, in preaching, and in administrative work. He bears the burden of the confidences of others to which he may not allude outside the counseling situation. One of the strongest temptations of the rabbi is to draw directly on his counseling experiences in his preaching. While they might add vividness and reality to his words, they are capable of embarrassing the individual concerned and can give rise to the suspicion that counseling relationships are being exploited.

Since the rabbi's role is not restricted to counseling, he must be able to compartmentalize his experiences and move from one area to another without confusing his different professional responsibilities. Role conflict is an almost inevitable stress for the rabbi. He requires exceptional insight and flexibility in order to detach himself from the private world of the congregant when he meets the same individual in an adult education class or in a committee meeting. The way he relates to individuals is determined by the particular situation and the different purposes of his encounters. At times awareness of individual problems must simply be suppressed so that the rabbi can avoid carrying over to more impersonal and objective situations the personal awareness he may have of special and private needs. He could easily become paralyzed as a leader were he to continue to be empathically involved with individuals whom he has counseled. He could not assert his ideas aggressively and speak for the group if he were always conscious of individual sensitivities and if he felt compelled to make allowance for the special needs of individuals whom he had previously encountered empathically in private meetings. Distinguishing between leadership and counseling situations calls for a degree of versatility and flexibility that is perhaps unique to the rabbinical profession.

The rabbi continues an ongoing relationship with the congregant even when counseling ceases, for he teaches, preaches, and ministers as the leader of the institution with which the congregant is affiliated. No one can expect the rabbi to maintain the intimate and personal quality of the dialogue in his subsequent interactions. The marriage counselor, the caseworker, or the therapist has no such challenge because his relationship to the client simply ceases when the purposes of private discussion have been accomplished.

Post-counseling relationships call for a delicate readjustment. For the congregant there is a period of uncertainty as he wonders about the trust he has invested in his spiritual leader. Will the rabbi relate to him as a problem or as a person? Will the rabbi feel he now has a particular hold on his loyalty? Some rabbis report that counseling is almost a disastrous experience because congregants, ashamed of having revealed their weaknesses to the rabbi, sometimes withdraw from the congregation to save face. They cannot cope with their ambivalent feelings towards the rabbi. Once having enjoyed his exclusive attention, they cannot share him with other members of the congregational family. They are concerned too that the rabbi may not accept them as independent personalities free to challenge him in discussion or disagree with his leadership. The problem can be minimized if the rabbi discusses it in advance with the congregant and assures him that each role has its own definition and its own limits. Moreover, the difficulty can be contained and limited if the rabbi avoids permitting the congregant to become too dependent upon him. By not assuming too much responsibility for the congregant, the rabbi can control the hostility and guilt that seem inevitable in more dependent relationships. It is not an uncommon experience for individuals to feel even freer to participate in the life of the community after learning to appreciate the integrity and character of the rabbi as an individual. At its best, counseling may lead to a recognition of the rabbi as being more than a functionary or a scholar remote from the actual concerns of man and community.

Transference

Some individuals react to the rabbi as a symbol of a father or a brother towards whom they once related with intense feelings of love or hate and often with a mixture of both. The process by which they transfer to a contemporary individual some attitudes derived out of their past is called transference. It is not possible to account for the intense reactions to religious leaders on the grounds of who they are or what they actually say or do without referring to the phenomenon of transference. Rabbis become figures for projected emotions, attracting accumulated feelings and dated emotions. As heads of congregational families, rabbis are symbolic fathers, givers of status and love, representatives of God, and embodiments of conscience. They are often cast into roles they would not choose. The wear and tear of transferred reactions can easily exhaust them emotionally, if they are unable to see that their very presence cues off reactions for which they are not responsible. Often they neither earn the intense love invested in them nor do they deserve the hostility directed against them. A distinction must be made between the rabbinical office and the personality of the rabbi. Those who fail to make the distinction can easily misinterpret the quality of the feelings expressed to them and develop self-images that simply do not correspond to reality. Unlike the psychoanalyst, the rabbi does not interpret transference reactions to the congregant. He becomes aware of them himself and does not react to them impulsively or defensively. He saves himself much personal discomfort when he identifies them properly and responds objectively to them.

In counter-transference, the rabbi responds to the congregant in ways that are equally unrealistic; he projects feelings on to him that are appropriate to members of his own family or to figures out of his own childhood. If the rabbi has unmet needs for expressing either love or hostility, he may find himself using counseling situations to work out his own problems. Rarely in rabbinical counseling are these needs expressed in an overt way in the form of acting out. What often happens is that the rabbi develops blind spots about the actual character of the congregant. He is blocked from gaining real knowledge of the other person because of his own tendency to project feelings and attitudes that are not relevant to the person he is meeting. He may feel himself threatened when no danger is involved or he may feel indulgent and uncritical when reserve is indicated. Self-knowledge can help the rabbi cope with the subtle risks of counseling. Like the hero defined in the *Ethics of the Fathers,* he must be capable of mastering his own passion.

There is some aspect of playing God in almost every counseling relationship. The rabbi, who not only counsels but preaches the word of God from the pulpit and invokes God's blessings in the priestly role is subject to feelings of omnipotence. Others assign him an authority he really does not have and he in turn may believe in his charisma. The rabbi can become too dependent upon emotional support from members of his congregation in any one of his several roles. He can easily lose sight of the fact that he may be attempting a superhuman role and come to feel himself swamped by the nearly impossible emotional demands of his position.

Other professions have developed techniques and resources for dealing with problems of transference and counter-transference. Professional workers consult with colleagues and often work under supervision of more experienced workers. It should be possible for the rabbi to review some of his own personal relationships with a skilled worker in human relations or check his own responses with a trusted colleague. In some cases psychological counseling may be needed. In any case, the rabbi requires the support of a peer group so that he can maintain professional standards in his often lonely and demanding work as a counselor.

Prophetic and Pastoral Roles

Can the rabbi combine the roles of prophetic critic and pastoral counselor? For some the answer is an unqualified negative. They see the rabbi essentially as a teacher and argue that no one man can integrate the two roles, one of which is essentially public and dramatic and the other private and far more passive. While some strain between the preaching and counseling roles is unavoidable, it should be possible for many rabbis to serve competently in each. Counseling is closely related to the priestly role with its concern for individual experience. If there is a decline of interest in the art of preaching, we must look elsewhere than in the so-called vogue of counseling. The total role of the clergyman in a secular society requires reevaluation. In the meantime preaching and counseling may be considered complementary rather than antithetical. The great Protestant preacher, Harry Emerson Fosdick, observed that he knew a sermon of his to be effective when it led people to come to him for personal consultation on the issues it raised. There is surely room in the rabbi's role for the large scale teaching involved in sermons as well as for the less directive type of guidance involved in counseling a single individual.

For some who are born leaders with a passion for public and dramatic communication, the counseling role is alien. They are temperamentally unsuited for the task. Their creative energies are evoked by the challenge of great ideas. They are brought to the peak of their powers by the presence of the audience. They cannot change their pace and accommodate themselves to the intense privacy of the dialogue. They want to work on a larger canvas and lack the patience for working on a miniature. The self-esteem of other rabbis is enhanced in their work with individuals. They seem guided by the principle that he who saves a single life has the merit of having saved the entire world.

The issue of prophetic versus counseling orientations can be understood in the light of the maternal and paternal roles. There is more of the maternal element in counseling and more of the paternal element in preaching but both activities have an aspect of each. In counseling the rabbi demonstrates a maternal concern for the individual; he is less judgmental and more accepting. He is concerned with conscience but he helps real feelings of responsibility to emerge by the slower process of listening and clarifying. There are stronger feelings of personal identification and support. The rabbi who would counsel offers patience and understanding. These attitudes become catalysts for change within the individual. It is entirely possible for the same rabbi to assume a more paternal and authoritative role when he preaches and teaches.

In his community leadership role the rabbi is more concerned with the group and the social conscience. He assumes aggressive moral leadership as the *mocheach* or moralizer, seeking to evoke feelings of guilt and responsibility. In his paternal role, the rabbi does not wait for the congregation to speak. He initiates the communication, arouses reactions, and persuades his congregation to accept his convictions. While he need not be moralistic or indignant, he is expected to dramatize moral values and exhort his group to conform to his standards. To carry over to the pulpit the more maternal orientation of the counseling session would be to inhibit the moral power and commitment which the preacher needs for his success as a change-agent. Preaching cannot be non-directive. In counseling, however, the rabbi takes his cue from the individual involved. He does not speak directly in terms of the ought. He is tentative and experimental in approach, feeling his way in an unstructured situation, always guided by the frame of reference of the other person. For everything there is an appointed time; the task of the rabbi is to choose between occasions when he will respond in the maternal mode and others when he will show more paternal leadership.

Relations with other Professionals

There may be room in the rabbinate for a religous specialist in counseling, a kind of synagogue professional who will devote himself exclusively to the small number of individuals seeking extended personal guidance. Such a rabbi, free from many of the distractions of general rabbinical service, could equip himself with technical training comparable to that of the caseworker or the psychotherapist and offer intensive counseling under synagogue auspices. There is some doubt however about the compatibility of such specialized counseling with the symbols and values associated with the religious institution. Such counseling might call for a more neutral environment. In the general pattern we can assume that even rabbis with special interests and qualifications for counseling will normally participate in other rabbinical activities. Counseling will continue to be part of a larger, cohesive role including teaching and priestly activities, to say nothing of administrative responsibilities.

In many cases, the rabbi's counseling consists of a single interview, a one-time encounter. At other times, a brief series of interviews is held. In situations calling for extended counseling, the rabbi can make referrals to caseworkers, to psychologists, and to psychotherapists. He cannot be expected to maintain a counseling practice and simultaneously fulfill all other demands on his time. To make a referral is to show respect for the congregant and is by no means an act of rejection. It is a reflection of self respect and not an admission of inadequacy.

Making a referral is an art in itself. A suggestion that further counseling is available made in even a slightly perfunctory way suggests to the congregant that the rabbi has ambivalent feelings about it. It is flattering to be sought for counsel and even if the situation presented is difficult and anxiety-provoking, there is often a reluctance to let go of the congregant and permit him to seek help elsewhere. There is more than a narcissistic involvement on the part of the rabbi. There is also the fear that suggesting a referral may be interpreted as an act of rejection. If the rabbi is genuinely persuaded that the congregant can be helped by more intensive and specialized counseling, he is more likely to feel that he is rendering an important service and that he is demonstrating real respect for the needs of the congregant when he makes the referral.

The rabbi obviously must understand what specialists in counseling have to offer. He must be able to interpret to the congregant the meaning of different types of counseling relationships. He himself must be persuaded that other professions have special competencies which can be useful to members of his congregation. To the degree that there is competition between the synagogue and the casework agency or the psychiatric clinic, it may be expected that referrals will not be effective. The rabbi and the counseling specialist need to be mutually informed regarding their respective areas of responsibility and service.

With insight and discrimination the rabbi can harmonize within himself the different roles of teacher, priest, preacher, and counselor. As a counselor, the rabbi has the opportunity of serving his people empathically. The dialogue takes its place with the sermon, the class, the pulpit, and the prayer-book, as an expression of Judaism as a way of life. As long as individuals need values by which to live, models of character with whom to identify, and relationships that yield meaning as well as courage, the rabbi has a unique role in modern Judaism. Placed in proper perspective, counseling can add immeasurably to the effectiveness of the rabbi.

II

Richard L. Rubenstein

The New Morality
and College
Religious Counseling

IT is extremely difficult to serve as a college chaplain without being constantly confronted with problems arising out of the current morals revolution. It may be a midnight call from a parent hoping the chaplain will have the address of a local abortionist or the seemingly casual inquiry of a student concerning how far to go. Sooner or later, there is hardly a sexual problem that does not come to the Hillel Director's attention.

The first prerequisite for effective religious counseling is that the college chaplain possess an informed conviction concerning what is appropriate in sexual matters. Without it, he can be of little help to students. There is nothing easy or automatic about this. It does not come rapidly or without much inner pain. It cannot be taught in the seminaries. There is inevitable self-involvement. What one counsels for others invariably reflects what one has come to regard as right and proper for oneself. A definite set of values is unavoidable.

There are also important differences between religious and

psychiatric counseling. Normally, a student seeks help from a clergyman because of a conflict between what he wants to do or is doing and his value structure. The student hopes that counseling will enable him to abide by his values or will aid him to exchange current norms for more realistic ones. *The student does not expect non-directive therapy from a clergyman.* He comes to a clergyman because the clergyman stands for something. An analyst or a psychiatric counselor need not reveal his own moral commitments in the therapeutic encounter. On the contrary, it is important that the therapist's values become irrelevant in the mind of the client. Such a posture of ethical neutrality is indispensable for therapy. It is impossible and undesirable in religious counseling.

In another place I have suggested that one of the functions of the college chaplain is to serve as a model with which students can test and form their own identities.[1] That does not mean that a successful chaplain will encourage students uncritically to imitate him or his values. I would stress the role he can play in offering the student a model for the testing of his own unique, developing identity. To function in this capacity, the clergyman must have done a great deal of work on his own inevitable problems. It is important that he resolve in his own life many of the moral and religious issues which remain matters of conflict and confusion for the student. He must have a flexible point of view developed out of inner feeling, commitment, and personal courage. The student will quickly intuit whether the chaplain holds his commitments as a result of fear of himself and his world or out of a realistic sense of confidence in his ability to manage his own life.

Counseling in the sexual area can be very threatening. Both the counselor and the client are self-involved to a far greater extent than in almost any other kind of counseling. This problem is especially important in counseling female students. The counselor must be open to what the girl is saying. The counselor must be aware of the fact that she may be

[1] Richard L. Rubenstein, "Hillel and the Ideologies of American Jewish Life", *The Reconstructionist*, January 7, 1966.

developing highly complex feelings, including sexual feelings, for him. This is the *transference* phenomenon which is
so decisive in psychotherapy. It is certainly present in religious counseling. Unless the counselor is capable of handling
it, he will become either defensive or over-involved in the
student. We must candidly recognize that there are real problems to be faced by a clergyman who is made privy to intimate details in the lives of young women. I cannot overstress
the need for personal insight as a prerequisite for effective,
objective counseling. Normally there is little danger that the
counselor will become sexually involved in his students, although that possibility can never entirely be dismissed. The
danger comes from the way in which the counselor handles
his avoidance of threatening involvements. It is not easy to sit
in a closed office confronted by a sexually disturbed, occasionally promiscuous female student. Warmth and objectivity are
both required. If one recognizes the strain, one is far less
likely to be affected by it than if one pretends it does not
exist.

My fundamental conviction in counseling is that sex is an
extremely serious business, involving our total personalities
at the deepest levels of our being. I realize that this conviction runs counter to the regnant mythologies of sex in American culture. These tend to regard sex primarily as a happy
form of recreation. The *Playboy* philosophy is less a molder
of culture than an indication of popular wish-fulfillment. It
must be reckoned with, especially in counseling. Students are
constantly confronted with images and attitudes which
largely underestimate the problematic and ironic aspects of
sex. This accords with the promptings of their bodies. Frequently, this is at odds with their inherited value structures
and their intuition that the sexual domain is far more complex than its presentation in the media of popular culture.
The idea that sex is evil had to be corrected. Unfortunately,
there is as little realism in the current negation of puritanism
as there was in the old puritanism. Realism demands that sex
be regarded as a matter of extraordinary significance and
complexity. A culture which sees sex as fun and games is just
as immature as a culture which regards it as evil.

In counseling sessions, I have found students concerned with practically every aspect of sex. These include pre-marital sex, masturbation, abortion, homosexuality, prostitution, extra-marital sex, frigidity, and impotence. Only rarely has a student come primarily for therapy; usually their objective was guidance and/or a dimunition of guilt. Very frequently I was convinced that they needed therapeutic help which I was not trained to give. In every instance where I felt therapy was indicated, I made a referral to a professional psychotherapist recommended by local psychiatrists. Nevertheless, the clergy does have an important role in counseling. Their counseling can be therapeutic. Not every student needs or is prepared for the kind of agonizing personal probing which is inevitable in the analytic situation. Many need intelligent and insightful guidance. This guidance can be therapeutic to the extent that the student is thereby enabled to reduce his conflicts in sexual matters.

Pre-marital Sex

The question of pre-marital sex arises with predicable regularity in religious counseling on campus. I have never been able to tell a student dogmatically that I either approve or disapprove of pre-marital sex. Instead, I have attempted to assist the student in understanding how much is really involved in a sexual relationship and to urge upon him caution lest he enter a relation for which he is emotionally unprepared. I have never offered any encouragement to a student to go further in a relationship than he was emotionally capable of handling.

On the other hand, I believe that even a clergyman who is opposed to pre-marital sex on religious grounds cannot be dogmatic about his opinions in counseling. Students will simply not pay any attention to a man who dogmatically counsels abstinence unless that is what they wanted to hear in the first place. Normally, they seek help because of the conflict between those forces which impel them toward abstinence—usually their inherited value-structures—and those needs of their minds and bodies which seek sexual gratification. When a clergyman dogmatically counsels abstinence, he usually proclaims his lack of sensitivity to what the student is going through. Usually, the student will conclude that he is not being heard and will seek help elsewhere.

When the student's conflict is understood and taken seriously, the counselor must seek to make the student understand that the real problem is never whether sex is right or wrong, but whether he or she is capable of handling the emotional entailments of the relationship. The student's greatest need is to realize how much of his total being is involved in *good sex* and therefore how very serious a matter it is.

I find that the rabbinic doctrine of *t'hyat ha-methim*, resurrection of the dead, is remarkably appropriate to contemporary sex ethics. Of all the religions of the Mediterranean world before the advent of Christianity, only Pharisaic Judaism believed in the resurrection of the dead. That meant that the rabbis were incapable of envisaging a life devoid of the body even in eternity. Unlike the Gnostics they did not divide reality into a good, *pneumatic* or spiritual existence and a bad corporeal existence. They correctly understood that all we have is our bodies and that all good and evil of which we are capable involves the body. There is enormous sanity in this perspective. It mitigates against the temptation to disassociate oneself from one's body and regard what one does with the body as not quite real. In terms of the ethics of sex, it suggests that *the investment of one's body in a relationship is in reality the investment of the total self.* Paradoxically, the more truly one values one's body, the more one realizes how a total commitment a good sexual relationship expresses.

I have met any number of students who have indulged in casual sexual relationships under the illusion that it was good clean fun that didn't matter much. I find, however, that when such students are honest about what transpired, they tell me that it was almost as if they weren't really there when it happened.

"I was there and yet I wasn't," one girl told me. "It was almost as if it were happening to another person. *I couldn't feel a thing.*"

We shall return to the theme of "I couldn't feel a thing." Very rarely do the lurid accounts of college sex say anything about this problem. Invariably, the most promiscuous girls are those least capable of real response. There is something pathetic about their hungry quest for gratifications which forever elude them. For a moment, I want to stress the sense of unreality and absence participants in these relations frequently report. It is easy for such students to go from one relation to another or to carry on multiple relations simultaneously. They are not really present in anything remotely resembling a genuine I-Thou relationship. Something psychotic takes place. There is a separation of mind and body. Where both mind and body are in harmony, it is difficult for the participants not to be come involved in each other. Normally students who are promiscuously involved need a different order of assistance than a clergyman can offer. What I am able to do for such students is to help them realize their need for therapeutic insight. Frequently, these students carry a very heavy burden of guilt which is all the more venomous because it is so difficult to acknowledge. I am sometimes able to make them see that their problem must be understood from the perspective of sickness and health rather than good and evil. Paradoxically, promiscuous students tend to be deeply cynical about the possibility of gratifying, responsible hetero-sexual relations. I often find that it is important to let the student understand that sex is more than an agonizing trap, that good hetero-sexual relations are possible for them. Unless the student has the vision that there is a better way, he has little motivation to seek it. It may sound odd, but an important aspect of the counselor's task is to encourage the student to believe in the possibility of good sex. There is a great deal of despair in promiscuous sex.

Many students see sex primarily as a way to release tension. They have little awareness of what they really seek in the sexual relationship. At the deepest level, the student seeks what we all seek, a source of love and comfort. Sex is a mode of relating to another human being. In it we dispense with such abstract modes of relationship as speech and intellectual concept. We restore to primacy our oldest mode of relating to others, direct bodily contact. Any intimate relationship involving bodily contact inevitably recalls our first source of love, our parents. One must have the wit and the insight deeply to know that the partner is not the parent. That is not always as simple as it may seem. We must help the student to understand that in sex we seek to recapitulate the oldest sources of love and basic trust in a manner appropriate to where we are in the time-table of life. That is an enormously serious matter. What we receive is capable of enabling us to face life with great confidence. When love is denied, the threat can be almost as all-pervasive as were the earliest denials of love in infancy. We have a name for good sex. It is love. The proliferation of hard, cold, seemingly unfeeling, but inwardly burning individuals in our culture bears witness to the hideous psychic warping which takes place when real love is denied. I doubt that many insights are as important to the student as the knowledge of how important good sex is.

Sexual contacts tend to be frequent among college students. Good sex is far less frequent. One of the most difficult aspects of the current freedom is that it encourages constant self-avoidance in sexual matters. Instead of probing within to discover what conflicts impede full gratification, failure to achieve gratification usually encourages an interchange of partners. Inevitably the same frustrations reassert themselves with the new partner. Students complain with depressing regularity of their inability to enjoy their relationships fully. There is a tendency toward quick gratification under adverse circumstance. Girls talk of being "left up in the air." Boys are often hardly interested in their partner's response. The "gang-bang" is a frequent fraternity activity. We would be far less sexually preoccupied society were we a more sexually gratified society. A college chaplain can go only so far in dealing with problems arising out of failure to obtain gratification. At present his best resource is a psychiatric referral.

There is no really adequate way of handling the problem of pre-marital sex in our culture. The gap between the age of biological and sociological readiness is not likely to be narrowed in our time. Given this gap, we shall have to muddle along with a difficult problem as compassionately and as insightfully as possible. Any course a young person elects has its special problems. Abstinence can be emotionally and psychologically difficult for some; a relationship lacking the full mutual commitment and social sanction of marriage will provide most young people with far more problems than they can usually intuit. I must confess that I am more aware of the problems than I am of viable pre-marital solutions. While I realize the inevitability of pre-marital sex in our culture, I am convinced that the traditional religious affirmation of the primacy of the marital relationship as the appropriate institution for good sexual relations remains completely on target. The counselor has a continuing role in upholding the centrality of marriage in our culture. Access to sexual partners has undoubtedly increased outside of marriage. I seriously doubt that the potentiality for gratifying love involving real commitment has grown outside of marriage.

Homosexuality

Every college chaplain confronts the problem of homosexuality among his students with dreary regularity. There is a real difference between students who seek help and hardened members of the "gay world." The student who seeks help doesn't want to remain homosexual. He usually feels guilty about his activities. He often understands his homosexuality to be an incomplete, infantile mode of sexual expression. When he comes to a chaplain, he is really saying "Help me!"

A clergyman is most helpful when he regards the student's homosexuality as a form of sickness rather than as a respectable alternative to hetero-sexual behavior. In counseling homosexual students I try to avoid adding to the student's burden of guilt. Those students who come for help are usually initially burdened by too much guilt. Nevertheless, I thoroughly disagree with those clergymen who believe they must lift the burden of guilt from the homosexual completely so that he is free to live as a homosexual without pangs of a guilty conscience. Students really want to know that there is a way out.

I do not believe that any clergyman, no matter how skilled, ought to depend upon his own counseling ability in cases dealing with homosexuality. His first objective should be to convince the student of his need for competent psychiatric assistance. At the same time, he must be both nonjudgmental and firm in the conviction that hetero-sexual sex, ultimately a full commitment within marriage, is the most desirable mode of sexual activity.

Frequently, students who are referred to psychiatrists keep in touch with the clergyman. The clergyman has to avoid a number of pitfalls in this parallel relationship. Much of what the student must uncover about himself is extremely painful and difficult to face. He may seek to avoid the pain of psychiatric probing by telling the chaplain how poorly the psychiatrist is handling his case or how the chaplain does a better job or how he no longer needs help. The role of the clergyman can only be to encourage the student to continue his therapy until both the student and the therapist agree that it is possible to terminate the encounter.

Masturbation

Occasionally, students express conflicts about masturbatory activity in counseling. Some degree of masturbation among unmarried college students is almost inevitable. It is unwise for the chaplain to heighten the student's feeling of guilt nor can he act as if masturbation were of no consequence. Auto-erotic manipulation involves a lack of real encounter with the other as Thou. To the extent that the student prefers it to the hazards and promises of a real encounter, the student is psychotic in sexual matters. The student cuts himself or herself off from others and dwells only in the solipsistic circle of the self. One girl told me that she was compelled to such activity several times a day. It was evident that auto-erotic activity was her mistaken way of warding off the anxiety involved in inter-personal relations. She had also had a number of sexual affairs, but like most of the girls who have discussed their pre-marital affairs with me, she was utterly incapable of full sexual gratification in the sexual act. She would inevitably have to finish what the boy began in the privacy of her own room. She was deeply disturbed by the fact that she derived greater pleasure out of what she did to herself than what occurred in her relationships. She was very fearful lest her inability to feel in sexual relations extend to marriage. She saw herself as marrying for the sake of security, feigning sexual satisfaction, and withdrawing totally within herself. She needed far more professional help than I was capable of giving her. She was unwilling to seek such help and I cannot report a happy resolution of her problem.

Abortion

The pill and the coil may be almost error-proof, but they are not proof against a girl who unconsciously desires a child no matter what the cost to herself or the child. I seriously doubt that many accidental conceptions take place any more. Conceptions do occur which are aborted in a variety of ways.

Few aspects of sex are as ugly as the abortion problem. The worst sufferers are students with relatively little means. Frequently inter-racial liasions result in unwanted pregnancies. I was told a year ago by an intelligent Negro student about the kinds of abortions attempted by students without money. These include the use of clothes hangers, emetics, and patronizing unsanitary facilities in the black ghetto usually resorted to by prostitutes. The description of some of the things which take place was quite sickening.

Occasionally, students faced with the need to do something about an unwanted pregnancy have consulted me. I am not at all sure I have been able to be of much help. The traditional Jewish attitude is hostile to abortion. I find myself bound by that attitude and also by the fact that abortion is normally a criminal procedure in the Commonwealth of Pennsylvania. Even if I believed that abortion were sometimes justified, there is no way in which I could be a party to an abortion under normal circumstances without violating the law. In spite of this, I have on occasion been approached by students, their parents, and their friends who wanted my assistance in securing a local abortionist. In every instance I have had no recourse but to suggest that the parties involved consult a physician to ascertain if there is any medical or psychiatric reason justifying a legal abortion. Beyond that, it is impossible for me to go. The problem is obviously worse for the poor than the rich.

In spite of my inability to honor a request for assistance in finding an abortionist, I am not happy with the alternatives. Where the parents are unprepared to accept responsibility for their own off-spring, they bring into the world a human being whose initial experience of the world is one of total parental rejection. That is an act of unparalleled emotional violence, albeit unintentional. I am convinced that a child ought not to enter the world under such circumstances, but I am equally convinced that there is no moral or legal justification for me to encourage abortion. I always come away from such situations with a renewed awareness of the sickness and ugliness of irresponsible sex.

Extra-marital Sex

One of the most important areas of discussion in the new morality is the problem of extra-marital sex. This is a matter of worry and concern to many students. They are aware of the difficulties involved in achieving a good marriage. When they inquire about the question of extra-marital sex, they are usually asking the question, "Can I achieve a good marriage?" Occasionally, but not frequently, a boy or girl finds himself involved in a marital triangle. When the subject is broached, I am convinced the counsellor must stress the utter seriousness and sanctity of marriage. Extra-marital relations must be interpreted as a failure in the marriage relationship. The sanctity of marriage hardly lends itself to liberal reinterpretation within a Jewish perspective. It is important to stress what a good marriage consists of, sexually and psychologically. For the sake of good, wholesome marriages, the clergyman must stress the psychological and physiological desirability of full mutual gratification by the marital partners. Failure to obtain full gratification must be regarded as a condition which demands rectification, if possible, within the marriage. I usually stress the counseling and psychotherapeutic agencies available in the community in the face of such a contingency. This is especially important with couples who contemplate marriage. I also stress the emptiness of substitute gratifications such as professional recognition or status achievement when a good marital relationship cannot be achieved. Above all, I emphasize the fact that adultery indicates a failure to achieve a good relationship and constitutes an unrealistic attempt to find love when the most appropriate institution for it fails.

The Need For Caution

I have tried to suggest in this discussion some of the complexities involved in counseling where sexual problems are involved. I have compared notes with psychoanalysts, marriage counsellors, gynecologists, and other clergymen. I find that men who have had any degree of experience in dealing with the conflicts arising out of sex tend to great caution and conservatism. Perhaps fifty years ago the overwhelming problem was that loosening an overly rigid sexual code. Today that problem is no longer of decisive importance. On the contrary, our problem comes from the opposite direction. There is very little left in the way of institutionalized norms which can give the individual guidance in sexual matters. No matter how infantile, unrealistic or limited a sexual response one seeks, a willing partner can be found. I am well aware of the fact that we can not restore the old norms, though I am somewhat less happy at their disappearance than many. The problem today is what we do with our freedom. If freedom leads to infantile acting out or neurotic pseudo-gratifications and a concomitant failure to achieve really meaningful and lasting relationships, that freedom will be worth little indeed. If freedom leads to enduring, committed relations between men and women for whom the deepest kind of sharing

life affords can become a continuing source of mutual renewal and growth in marriage, then it will have proven more
than worth the risks it entails. Nevertheless, as I conclude I
must confess that I cannot be entirely optimistic. Human
beings are capable of the greatest folly precisely where they
are most deeply involved. That is why I cannot help but look
back upon the broken grandeur of Torah with more than a
little sadness. Those who were guided by its norms may not
have achieved the depth of mutual gratification inner insight
can afford; they were nevertheless defended against their
anarchic inclinations. They managed to muddle through
without reaching the heights or touching the depths of what
is now possible. I suspect that in the long run fewer people
were hurt that way.

I catch myself. Looking back is futile. We are, as Sartre has
commented, condemned to be free. Let us make the most of
it with least hurt to ourselves and those we love.

III

Albert I. Gordon

The Rabbi
and the Problem
of Intermarriage

CAN a rabbi to whom young people and their parents turn for counsel in situations that involve intermarriage and related subjects really be objective? Is it possible for an ordained religious leader, representing a particular set of beliefs, practices, and a way of life, to offer counsel and guidance that is free from a distinctive bias? The answer is obviously, "No!" I do not believe that those who turn to the rabbi for counsel really expect what passes for "objectivity". What persons really seek is guidance from a man in whose basic integrity they believe and whose experience in this particular area of their concern is greater and more varied than that of most professional counselors. It is precisely because the rabbi has a positive religious philosophy that he may be in the very best position to counsel, especially in the field of interfaith marriage.

The rabbi can hardly be objective in his attitude toward the problem of intermarriage because he is called upon to seek every proper means to perpetuate the faith of his

[39]

Fathers, Judaism—and to perpetuate the Jewish People, through whom this faith can live on. He must be, as were his Fathers, concerned with the survival of the Jewish People on its highest level, seeking always to strengthen loyalty to a distinctive way of life.

This is not to say that the rabbi should be unconcerned with the personal lives of the individuals who comprise that People. Judaism has made its concern for the individual, his personal happiness both in and out of marriage, crystal clear. We recognize and, indeed, call attention to the fact that individuals are dependent upon each other. We are part of a people and of a society. Just as we reap the benefits that accrue from our societal relations, so we suffer the consequences of society's failures or insufficiencies.

Judaism teaches too that in marriage, man and woman complement each other, adding a spiritual quality that cannot be acquired in a single state. Marriage is spoken of, in Judaism, as *Kiddushin*. It is a state of sanctity and holiness given two humans who may find fulfillment in each other. According to Judaism, marriage is a spiritual relationship. Judaism declares that if these two live within the bounds set for them by their Torah, their lives will complement each other. Each will find fulfillment.

It is the rabbi's duty to explain this concept to all young people who seek to enter into the holy bonds of matrimony. He has a very special duty and obligation to make this interrelationship clear to those persons who turn to him for counsel and guidance when the possibility of interfaith marriage is involved. This is why the rabbi cannot, if he is to be true to his calling, accept an intermarriage situation without raising many serious and all-important objections. The rabbi cannot be objective!

But it is doubtful too that even a non-religiously oriented counselor can be utterly objective. For no man lives in an utter vacuum, free from ideals, ideas, values, and beliefs. Hence, the rabbi (or any other cleric in any other organized religious group) need not apologize or offer excuses for the fact that he has personal views and convictions on the matter of intermarriage that can hardly be called "objective."

However, whatever his convictions, however strong his views, the rabbi-counselor should, above all else, seek to be both understanding of the problems that are being presented to him and as patient and gentle as he can possibly be in seeking a solution for them. No two situations in the area of intermarriage problems, as in other areas, are exactly alike. Each problem must be dealt with as unique and distinctive.

Thirty-eight years in the rabbinate have convinced me that the number of situations and problems for which unequivocal clear answers involving a simple "yes" or "no" answer can be given are remarkably few. Rather, as the years roll by, most of the situations with which I am concerned these days, seem to involve varied shades of grey rather than shades that are black or white.

The rabbi-counselor requires above all else the ability to listen carefully and understandingly even if he is not always in agreement with the points of view that are being expressed.

What types of intermarriage situations does the rabbi generally encounter and how ought he to respond to them?

In most instances, it is the parents of some youth who is facing a potential intermarriage situation who are the first to communicate with the rabbi, seeking his assistance in the prevention of such a marriage.

Sometimes, one wonders why certain of these parents are so aghast at the very thought of an interfaith marriage for their own religious and cultural ties to Judaism and the Jewish People are often negligible if not non-existent. However much these parents may have failed their children by providing inadequately for them as Jews, it is the rabbi's duty to listen to these parents as sympathetically as possible. It is not his duty to pass judgment on them or even to chastise them verbally. There is nothing to be gained by such an action.

The primary concern must be directed toward the effort of assisting the youth, the child of these parents, to understand that the Jewish People and, consequently, Judaism may suffer because of his or her move. I believe that the number of Jews in the world who identify themselves as Jews is already so small that we can ill afford the loss of a single person who has the potentials for living a positive Jewish life. Because the chances for such a life are considerably reduced through intermarriage, I would offer whatever assistance I can to such parents and to their offspring, but—on one important condition—the young person himself (or herself) must communicate with me and invite my cooperation and counsel. The request for an appointment must come from the person who is directly involved. For only then can the rabbi be sure, in some degree at least, that he is in communication with someone who is seeking counsel and guidance rather than an argument.

Situations involving the possibility of intermarriage frequently occur in families where, from all external appearances, the children have been reared on a positive Jewish plane. There are many such families whose respect and observance of the Sabbath and Festivals is marked; whose children have received a better than average Hebrew School education; where the love of the Jewish people and concern for its perpetuation are clearly evident.

In these families, too, intermarriage often makes its inroad. It is propinquity, the nearness of Jew and non-Jew to each other, the vastly increased opportunities that exist in our society for direct contact with persons of other faiths, rather than "escapism" or "rebelliousness" against parents or Judaism that creates the situations that ultimately give rise to interfaith marriages.

In these cases too, the rabbi should seek to know as much as possible about these parents, their family life, and more particularly, about the relations that exist between parents and their way of life and that of their children. One must not take it for granted that because parents are themselves devout and devoted Jews, they are necessarily good or even understanding parents. In most cases, one interview with parents will suffice to provide a considerable degree of understanding concerning the nature and attitudes of these parents and their children.

The rabbi should not assume that any judgment he may have tentatively reached, as a consequence of a meeting with parents, is necessarily correct. He should attempt as deftly as possible, to obtain some evaluation on this score from the youth who is being interviewed. He may find that whatever the religious orientation and general cultural and social level of the parents, there has often been a marked failure on the parents' part to transmit their values to children. Sometimes children are deeply resentful of parents and their method of teaching their values. Rebellion though not as manifest as in a generation gone by is still evident in our day.

When the appointment is made with the youth who is seeking counsel, I urge that he or she visit me alone. The discussion under this circumstance is freer and easier, not only for the youth, but for the rabbi as well. I always make the point that, in this first meeting, at least, it is best to discuss the issues and problems involved without making any judgment or evaluation in even the slightest degree of the non-Jewish potential partner to the proposed intermarriage. Thus, the question of liking or disliking that person cannot enter into the discussion. If, however, there are to be further meetings, both parties should be invited to attend. In most instances, this suggestion is accepted without debate. If, however, there is a demand that I meet with both young people at this first visit, I will generally accede.

At the first meeting, I try to obtain as complete a personal history of the youth as possible. This would include, not only schools attended, relations with parents, siblings and extended family, but also information concerning the psychological and social responses to family, society, religion, and issues of the day, including civil rights and social action. A few questions are usually sufficient to elicit a niagara-like volume of response and reactions that help me to make a few tentative conclusions as to the nature of the problem and if or how I can deal with it.

In all cases, I try to be as gentle, as patient and as understanding as possible. But this does not mean that I have forgotten that my basic and primary interest is the preservation of Judaism and the Jewish People. If I forget this all-important fact, I believe that I fail as a rabbi.

How should a rabbi, in his role as a counselor, address himself to a youth who declares that he is in love with a person of another faith and appears to be inclined to enter into an interfaith marriage?

If, in response to my preliminary questions and discussion, I find that the youth has a deeply rooted love and respect for his parents and family, I try to have the interviewee tell me what effect such a marriage might have upon his loved parents and family. Further, if the facts warrant, I seek to have the youth evaluate the love his parents bear for their religious heritage. Through a series of reminders of the manner in which Sabbaths, Festivals, and Holy Days were celebrated in his home, it is my hope that these pleasant memories can be stirred sufficiently to cause him to appreciate how much these distinctly Jewish rites mean, not only to parents, but actually to the interviewee! If, further, the unique *values* that are represented by these observances can be impressed upon his mind, I will, at least, have made the position and meaning of both family and religion more relevant and meaningful.

Further, I discuss certain facts concerning the history of the Jewish People that bear particularly on the issue of our survival. I point out that for many centuries the physical survival of the Jewish people has actually been at stake, not only because of the blood baths our people has been obliged to endure, resulting in the tragic decimation of this people of which we (he and I) are a part, but in the subsequent loss of influence of its distinctive values as well. I recommend a reading (or rereading) of a one-volume history of the Jews with particular emphasis upon the life of the Jewish people since the days of our Emancipation in the past several centuries. I stress the story of the destruction of the six million during World War II, the martyrs of the Warsaw Ghetto and how, as a consequence of that holocaust, only approximately eleven million Jews remain alive in the entire world. I indicate why the loss of a single individual Jew or a family of Jews has tragic consequences in that it affects the ultimate survival of the Jewish People. At this point, I usually recommend that Dr. Abba Hillel Silver's excellent book, *"Where Judaism Differed"* (MacMillan) be studied with the hope that these distinctive values and their significance be understood and appreciated.

It is generally agreed that a marriage that does not include a similarity of religious background or, at the very least, agreement on matters of religious concern, is more likely to fail than a marriage of a couple possessing the same faith. Nor does the fact that some young people declare that they have in common an indifference to religion assure a happy marriage. Two zeroes are still equal to zero! Whereas, sociological studies indicate that two to three times as many marriages fail when the parties to the marriage are of different religions, the same sociologists indicate that the ratio of marital failures actually increases when neither party has any religious affiliation.

Further, it ought to be noted that however minor the role of religion may appear to be in one's life, there may come times when the association of religion to the life of the family has very special meaning. The young man for whom the Passover Festival has great meaning, not only because of the values represented by the Festival but more particularly because it is the season in which members of the family assemble in joyous fellowship to recite the *Haggadah,* the narrative of the exodus of the Hebrews from Egypt, or to chant the traditional melodies and eat of the special Festival foods, is not likely to enjoy the prospect of non-participation in the Passover Seder. Nor is he likely to feel that the Christmas or Easter Festivals are other than foreign to him. However much in love young people may be, however much they may be concerned with each other's happiness, they can hardly cut themselves off completely from their own families and cultural heritage. Any attempt to do so is more than likely to increase differences and dissensions between them.

Further, if a mixed marriage takes place, (in which each party retains his and her own religious affiliation) what is likely to happen when children become part of the family? Is it fair to deprive children of any religious training? Is it right that they should be placed in the embarrassing position of having, at a later point in their lives, to make a choice between the religion of their father and that of their mother?

If, as a consequence of these choices, there could be some assurance that one world, free from inequity and injustice, could be secured, there would be some reason to give pause, even serious consideration to such a possibility. In my view, there is no indication to date that interfaith marriage is even likely to produce such a world. Why then sacrifice the very religious values which, if lived by, may more effectively produce the kind of world we desire?

I cite the general approach to the problem of intermarriage that I follow in most cases. It should be noted that I refrain from any approach to the interviewee that suggests or implies a threatening attitude; that declares that parents ought to threaten to cut off contact with an intermarried son or daughter; that infers that he or she is an outcast and a pariah.

Certain of my Orthodox rabbinic colleagues have taken exception to my approach. They state that my failure to make clear that intermarriage is a traitorous act insofar as Judaism and the Jewish People are concerned, only tends to increase the possibility of intermarriage. I cannot accept their views. I see in them a failure to come to terms with the Twentieth Century in which they live. On the contrary, because our children are so very dear and precious to us, I cannot urge any parent, no matter what the circumstance, to establish any barrier between himself and his children. However we may grieve, the deliberate and self-imposed separation of parent from children is, I believe, a sinful act.

There are occasions when, after a meeting with two young people of differing faiths, I tentatively conclude that there is the likelihood that if the non-Jewish party were formally converted to Judaism, accepting this faith and the People in all sincerity, that marriage would have a fairly likely opportunity to succeed. I do not advocate conversion very often. No matter how exact and detailed a course of study is required or how many discussions are entered into, I am not convinced that these converts could shed the ideas or attitudes they acquired in their childhood and accept completely new ideas and values as if these were nothing more than the change-over from one garment to another. Yet, on occasion, I do believe that I see such a person. Inasmuch as Judaism provides the means, i.e. conversion, I believe that it is right and proper that it be utilized correctly. I know of cases where conversion to Judaism, even though it appears to have resulted from the desire to marry a Jew or Jewess, has resulted in the acquisition of a fine, positive Jew, in addition to helping assure the success of a particular marriage.

Let it be clear, however, I do not advocate the uncontrolled use of conversion. Generally, I do, in fact, oppose it. But I would be both naive and unfair if I denied that, in certain particular cases and especially when the rabbi has had every opportunity to really come to know both young people intimately and, mindful of his great responsibility as the preserver of the Faith and a People, that conversion may prove unsuccessful.

However, if conversion is to be undertaken, in my view, it ought to be traditional in every way possible. It ought to include a long and intensive period of study of Judaism—its history, its ritual, its theology, and the study of Hebrew as the language of prayer. It ought to include the traditional immersion ceremony, the circumcision rite in the case of a male, the formal test of the knowledge and understanding of Judaism in the presence of a Tribunal, the adoption of a Hebrew name, and the formal documentation of the occasion. "Conversions made easy" are less likely to effect either a successful Jewish marriage or the serious adoption of the way of life we know as Judaism.

I am convinced that if the idea of a formal conversion is agreed upon, the rabbi who will serve as instructor should insist that the Jewish as well as the non-Jewish party involved should jointly undertake the study of Judaism. Experience has taught me that when *both* persons study Judaism together, and have the opportunity to talk freely to the rabbi about their uncertainties and doubts, to raise questions and elicit responses, to talk also, about their hopes and aspirations in each other's presence, that healthy, meaningful ties are created that augur well for both the marriage and Judaism.

If, in my conversations with the young people, the non-Jewish party should refuse to consider the possibility of conversion for himself, I would then be obliged to refuse to consider further, discussions on the subject of intermarriage with either of the parties.

If, however, the idea is acceptable and if I know that the Jewish parents are utterly opposed to the idea, I would, as gently as possible, seek to help them change their mind, provided I, in my own mind, am as convinced as I can be that *this* marriage is really right.

If, too, the young people are still in their teens, or obviously immature despite their years, or are economically dependent upon the support of parents, I would dissuade these young people from a consideration of marriage or from contemplation of conversion to Judaism by the non-Jewish member of the couple.

No rabbi, whether he be young or old, whether he is experienced as a counselor or not, dares regard himself as infallible in his judgments. He can, in this type of situation as in most others, only conjecture, or at best, offer an educated guess about what may happen to these two young people. He ought only on the rarest of occasions to offer to proceed with preparation for conversion when parents remain bitterly opposed to it.

There are those situations in which two young people of different religious faiths, one of whom is Jewish, invite a rabbi to officiate at their marriage. These two intend also to invite a non-Jewish clergyman who represents the faith of the other person in the proposed marriage to officiate as well. Sometimes the couple, in their ignorance, will suggest that both rabbi and minister officiate together. At other times, the suggestion is made that the rabbi might officiate at one ceremony at which the Jewish family are present, while on another day and at another time, the Protestant or Catholic clergyman would officiate at the second ceremony. It is assumed that this will "satisfy" the several families involved.

Some years ago, a young couple, the man, Jewish and a university professor, and the girl, a Baptist and a graduate student at the University, invited me to officiate at such a marriage. After careful probing, I discovered that the young couple had no religious orientation but were anxious to please their respective parents and families by following such a procedure. I pointed out, gently but firmly, that, as a rabbi, I could officiate only at marriages in which *both* bride and groom were Jewish. I indicated that it was my responsibility to preserve the faith of the Jew and the Jewish People. Under the circumstances, I pointed out, I could hardly permit myself to officiate unless the non-Jewish party to the marriage would agree to formal conversion to Judaism. Furthermore, I added, such a conversion would require months of careful study of Judaism that would then have to be followed by a formal conversion ceremony. After these requirements had been met, the religious ceremony might then take place.

The young couple, astounded by these proposals, made it clear that I, the rabbi, was regarded as one of the means whereby the respective families would be placated. When I made it equally clear that the rabbi was not to be "used", the couple were very unhappy. But, I believe I had helped these young people to understand the nature of the rabbinical function and duty.

The rabbi-counselor is no miracle-worker. He cannot solve everyone's problems. However, he should have a particular orientation that must not be ignored or even minimized in importance. He is a religious leader. It is his duty and sacred obligation to preserve his Jewish heritage—its ideals, its values, and its distinctive ways. He has the duty to strengthen the spiritual ties of Jews, to bring them closes to their Torah. In these days, the number of persons who fail to recognize this basic duty, who come to the rabbi seeking his counsel and guidance, has increased. That does not mean that the rabbi, flattered by this attention, should fail to respect his responsibility to help preserve Judaism and the Jewish People. To be permissive is to perform a disservice to our ancient tradition. Yet each person who turns to the rabbi for counsel is a child of God, to be dealt with gently, understandingly, and kindly. If the rabbi can be of assistance to anyone and yet remain steadfast and firm in his determination to preserve that Faith, let him, by all means, do so.

IV

Irwin M. Blank

Counseling the
Aged and
Their Families

It is the fear of abandonment which is the recurring motif both in the literature treating of the problems of the aging and in the problems presented to the rabbi in his role of counselor. The fear of abandonment is expressed not only by the aging individual but by the younger members of his family as well, those who through the years have always regarded him as a "tower of strength" "someone to lean on." Thus, the fear of abandonment is an all pervasive one, felt by all who participate in the ongoing flow of history.

In an age which places particular value on work (a Protestant motif; Judaism values study above work) the practice of a mandatory retirement age virtually socializes the process of abandonment by informing an individual that in the eyes of society he is no longer suitable for his work, and therefore, he is no longer to be considered a productive member of society. What greater humiliation than to be judged by one's society as being useless. It is understandable that the

[51]

fatality rate should be so high upon retirement of individuals who previously showed no serious disorders. Thus, at an age when the individual may be equipped to bring to bear not only the skill which he has developed through the years but the wisdom of mature judgement to his chosen work, society arbitrarily rules him as useless. In an age which overvalues work, this is virtually declaring an individual a non-person.

In counseling those who feel abandoned by society because society has deprived them of the right to work, the rabbi may certainly draw from Jewish tradition which emphasizes Torah, the study of God's truth, rather than the production of goods. Success, as defined in the business world, as the ability to produce goods and acquire income, is not at all a value in Jewish thought. Work is for the purpose of providing the individual with what he needs in order to live so that he may be free to fulfill the commandments. Work, insofar as one is able to perform it, is for the purpose of not becoming a charge on the community. But, the ability to work is not to be the measure of whether or not one is a worthwhile human being.

Thus, the rabbi has the responsibility of reorienting the individual who is depressed and adrift because of retirement towards a more Jewish scale of values. There are opportunities for activity which may be open to the individual whose new found leisure is intolerable. These might include service occupations, either for pay or as a community volunteer, or opportunities to serve as a consultant in one's former full time work. But, it is the basic problem of evaluating one's self in terms of one's ability to work, or even more precisely, society's evaluation of one's ability to work, which is the recurring one. However, the psychiatrist or the psychologist may deal with this problem, the rabbi can certainly deal with this in terms of Jewish values and Judaism's evaluation of the individual—an evaluation which does not center upon the ability to work but rather on the extent to which the individual fulfills his capacity to be a human being as evidenced by his fulfillment of the commandments. Just what the nature of those commandments are will of course depend upon the particular philosophy of the rabbi as expressed by his commitment either to Orthodox, Conservative or Reform Judaism.

It is also possible for rabbis to examine with business leaders this socially acceptable means of abandoning the aged with the purpose of determining whether or not mandatory retirement is really a sound business concept or simply a cultural convention which has been permitted to go unchallenged. One thing is clear. The concept of mandatory retirement has wrought great havoc with our aging. In the counseling situation, we may be able to help the individual to restructure his value system so that it is more closely in accord with Judaism's scale of values. In the community we may be able to counsel with business leaders in order to have them restructure their business practices.

The death of one's friends or of one's mate is oftentimes interpreted as abandonment. How often does the rabbi hear at a funeral the bereaved cry out, "Why have you left me?" The individual upon whom one has lavished love, care, and concern has died and the response to that fact may be the feeling that one is slowly but surely being set adrift in a strange and unwelcoming world. It has often been observed that the mourner's meal with family and friends following the burial and the social visiting during the *shiva* period can serve to offset this feeling of being abandoned. But, it is also true that when the mourning period is over, family and friends must return to their concerns and normal routines and more often than not are not able, do not care to or are not sufficiently sensitive to restructure their lives to include the bereaved. One need not dwell at length upon the intense loneliness felt by widow or widower until such time as it is possible for them to restructure their lives so that they are able to invest their interest and love in another. The rabbi can be of help by making it possible for the bereaved to discuss plans for forming new friendships or the possibility of remarriage without running the risk of meeting with the ambivalence or outright hostility which the widow or the widower often experiences from his children. It sometimes happens that the rabbi himself, because of his expressions of interest and concern, becomes the focus for the investment of friendship and love for the lonely bereaved. How the rabbi receives this investment will be determined by his feelings for the individual, but more importantly, the rabbi's response should be determined by his understanding of what the individual is doing with the rest of his life. For ultimately, the rabbi has his own family, friends, and needs. To mislead the bereaved into believing that the rabbi is prepared to make an emotional investment larger than that which he is truly prepared to make can only repeat the process of abandonment which brought the bereaved to the rabbi to begin with.

The decline of physical capacities may also contribute to the fear of abandonment. The realization that one is dependent upon others for certain services and for the carrying out of certain activities which formerly could be realized independent of assistance can lead to the fear that one will be abandoned and therefore, helpless. "What will I do if there is no one to help me?"Thus, to avoid the possibility of being helpless, the individual may limit his activities even further and withdraw increasingly into a passive existence. Program directors of senior citizens groups are discovering that the elderly can do much more than was previously realized. Hence, we find senior citizens groups featuring travel programs, swimming groups, painting classes, all of which involve physical activities. Physical checkups to determine just what one can or cannot do are helpful both to the aging and their families in order to have some realistic understanding of the range of possibilities in the matter of physical activity and independence. Physical checkups are helpful in coming to a realistic understanding of what the individual can do in order to guide him towards a more active program, in order to allay his fears of becoming too dependent on others, and in order to counsel those who live and work with him so that they will not permit him to become dependent in areas which he can handle himself. We most certainly want to protect our aging, but we do not want to make them dependent in areas in which they need not be.

There is another kind of abandonment, the abandonment which the aging feels concerning his culture. "Children didn't behave that way in my day." "They don't write songs the way they used to." "You don't look like a rabbi." Thus, the aging have a sense that history has passed them by and the familiar signposts by which they recognized their world have been repainted. Some are able to evaluate these changes in a fairly objective way, recognizing that in the world with which they identify there was good and bad as there is now. Others interpret these changes not in terms of the changes but rather as an indication that they are now strangers in the world and perhaps have outlived their welcome. On the other hand, the concepts of those around them, may keep them from vital engagement in the world as it is. "How undignified for a grandmother to behave that way." "Grandfathers are not supposed to have sexual desires." Thus, the feeling of being abandoned by one's culture may be the result of being unable to objectively evaluate one's culture or the imposition of the culture of concepts of what the aged are supposed to be like or not supposed to be like which are unrelated to the real needs and desires of the aging. Our concept of "The dignity of the hoary head" may be forcing our aging into nonengagement with life and frustrating their desires to satisfy legitimate needs and desires. Thus, their feeling of abandonment is realistic. Because they have arrived at a certain age in life, they are being abandoned. They are being abandoned as people.

But, there is the other side of the coin, the abandonment which the children of the aging sometimes feel. This is something akin to Jacob's intense desire to wrest a blessing from his aged father and Esau's furious response when cheated out of the blessing. The father whom we knew as a tower of strength or the mother who was always looking out for our welfare may no longer be that tower of strength or able to do all the little things which warmed us. Hence, the child may feel abandoned. "My mother cares only about herself, she never thinks of me." "My father can't seem to come to a decision about anything."

We have been suggesting that there are many areas of satisfaction open to the aging which will make it possible for them to maintain an active engagement with life, and that these areas of engagement should not be cut off from them either because of their own misunderstanding or the misunderstanding of others of their capacities or because of cultural stereotyping of the aged.

The book of *Ecclesiastes* in our Sacred Literature reveals for us the mind of a man who is coming to grips with his finiteness, who knows and sees with utmost clarity that life is quickly drawing to an end.

If the contemplation of the limitation of one's capacities or cultural supports is distressing, how much more so the contemplation of non-being. *Ecclesiastes* makes us aware of how the awareness of the nearness of death and its inevitability may cast the taste of ashes over all of life's experiences. *Ecclesiastes* seeks for that which will bring him a sense of ultimate fulfillment for he feels that whatever he has experienced thus far is transient and because it is transient, as it must be because of his own finiteness, it is therefore unsatisfying. Thus, he challenges the value of sensual experiences, work, the acquisition of knowledge. There is nothing to indicate that *Ecclesiastes* is married or has a family. But, one would guess that even if he were, he would ultimately find the satisfactions of wife and family unfulfilling for they too are transient. *Ecclesiastes* is generally referred to as the gentle cynic. It would be closer to the truth to describe him as terribly depressed, depressed by the awareness of the approach of death which he regards as defeat. Thus, if life is not eternal (In *Ecclesiastes* we find no indication of a concept of after life) then nothing man experiences can be worthwhile or deeply satisfying. We often find this sense of despair in the aged who wonder whether life is really worth it, whether what they have achieved is worthwhile because they feel their powers waning and know that death is near at hand. Thus, they evaluate what they have experienced or what they have done in terms of their ability to continue the experience.

Belief in an after life may offset these feelings of despair.

But, perhaps what is more significant is the need to establish a sense of community in the individual who sees no continuity, hence, no worth in the fact that he has lived and done. Judaism places considerable emphasis on the deed. Part of that emphasis derives from our belief that man is a historical creature. He makes history. He achieves not only personal salvation but the salvation of the world through history and in history. Thus, each of us can contribute to that process of achieving salvation by the performance of the *mitzvoth*. No more, no less is expected of us. We may conclude from the fact that women and children are excluded from the performance of certain *mitzvoth*, or at least these commandments are not mandatory for them, that one is only expected to do what one can do and that having done that, has made a significant contribution to the world. The point, however, is to feel at one with the world, to have a sense of community with it.

If one's worth is to be established only by one's ability to live, then, we are all worthless for death must claim us all. If, however, we have done what we could do and are doing what we can do with conviction, this must have an impact on the world. Thus, one never really leaves the world having been in it and having fulfilled the commandments.

We hear so much concerning alienated man because the problem of community is a general problem and not limited to the aged. In a world where war has become more and more impersonal and destruction more and more horrifying, it becomes increasingly difficult to feel a sense of community. But, for those who can still count on having a goodly number of years to live there is still the hope that man will come to his senses. For the aging and the aged who realistically cannot envisage many more years, both the approaching end of life and the possibility that the world will destroy itself conspire to create a total sense of alienation. Thus, one cannot even be certain that one's children and one's children's children will carry on that impulse which we set in motion during our lifetime. The problem in our age is compounded by the very real threat of nuclear destruction. One might accept the fact

of his own death. The possibility that his children and grand-
children, the world may be destroyed is that much more difficult to accept.

But, having said that Judaism believes in man as a historical being, and that the course of history is not inevitable, the
responsibility is man's to make whatever impact he can on
the flow of those events. We do not speak now of the senile
and those whose physical and mental deterioration is so great
that they cannot participate in any transactions. We speak of
the aging whose awareness of the approach of death depresses
and paralyzes them from further active engagement with life.
The rabbi can try to help them maintain an ongoing sense of
community and awareness of the very real impact they do
and can have.

Thus, the goal in helping those feel abandoned or in fact
are abandoned is to develop feelings of worthwhileness based
either on what one has done or on what can do.

For the children and for those who work with the aged,
the challenge is to resolve some of our own inadequate ways
of thinking of the aged. This may include the inability to
overcome our idealization of our parents, our continuing dependence upon them for approval or new blessings, our
stereotyped thinking concerning that which is appropriate or
inappropriate behavior for the aged e.g. in dress, heterosexual
relationships, physical activities.

The rabbi sees the problem of idealization of the parent in
those situations where the child is unable to accept the situation in which it is now the parent who is realistically dependent upon the care which he should receive from the
child, bringing about a reversal of roles. The child may be
resentful of the new demands placed upon him. He may feel
his own foundation somewhat shaky in that his own dependent needs are being frustrated. He may be unable to recognize or accept that his parent is no longer a "tower of
strength".

There is another way in which the rabbi sees the idealization of the parent—in the tensions arising in the three generation house or when a child who is now a parent is unable

to establish limits for a parent he feels is too involved in his life. It seems likely that the problem is the child's rather than that of the aging parent. It is the child who is unable to assert his own maturity and make it stick. He is unable to do so because he is still seeking approval although he resents what he now considers to be domination. The rabbi, in his role of counselor, may himself be subject to this kind of pressure from an elderly person. And rather than maintain an objective view of the person coming to him for counseling, he may find himself seeking approval as he might from his own parent.

The problem of idealization is also present in the matter of deciding upon the advisability of having the parent become a resident in a nursing home. The feeling that one is "putting the parent away" may be the result of being unable to recognize that the parent requires the kind of medical supervision and general care which cannot be given by the family or cannot be given without damaging emotional cost to all affected by the additional pressure. It may be true that for some children, they are in effect "putting the parent away" and using the dependence of the parent as an occasion to express hostility, to pay off old scores. But, it is also true that for many this is only realistic solution to a steadily deteriorating situation. This is function of the rabbi—to help those involved discuss all considerations involved in the most realistic way possible.

This discussion should certainly include the information that there is the possibility that upon admission to a nursing home, deterioration may be accelerated. Whatever the decision, it should be based upon what the present situation requires not upon unresolved parent-child relationships.

The present situation includes the level on which the aged person is functioning or could function with some assistance such as a companion, practical nurse, should this assistance be required. The present situation also includes financial considerations, cost of assistance as compared with cost of nursing home.

There is also the situation where although physically capable of being independent or relatively responsible, the aged person places a serious emotional burden on the family because of his inability to establish a workable relationship with the other members of the family. This may be due to the outcropping of old emotional problems long quiescent or the development of new problems.

But, there is also the very real possibility that the preparedness of the child to place the aging parent in a home is simply the result of not wishing to exert one's self to assume responsibility for another and to shirk that responsibility which quite properly rests with the family by relinquishing it to an institution.

Where the aging person requires the kind of intensive care and supervision which the individual family cannot realistically be expected to expend, except at great financial and emotional cost to itself, then a thorough exploration of the facts and the attitudes involved will reassure the child of the necessity and the wisdom of his decision.

But, where the family can and should assume responsibility for the care of their aging, then the rabbi must assume the counseling responsibility of helping them understand what it is they are avoiding and what inappropriate goal they are pursuing in wanting to admit the aged member to a home. Just as a sense of worth should not depend on the ability to work, it should not depend on the state of one's health. One should be able to maintain one's place within the family circle even if this involves an additional expenditure of emotional energy or financial resources over and above that normally required to maintain an ongoing relationship between two relatively independent people.

Although we acknowledge the need for institutionalization, we also acknowledge the need for assuming responsibilities which should be assumed by the family of the aged in maintaining him within his accustomed environment.

We have already indicated the availability of senior citizen programs and nursing homes for the aged. There are also senior citizen residences which are more in the nature of hotel accommodations offering special facilities and programs for the aging. The rabbi has the responsibility of familiarizing himself with the facilities and programs available in his community, requirements for eligibility, scope of the program and facilities, and cost to the participant and/or his family.

We have also spoken of two values foisted upon us which are not in the scale of Jewish values, the first being that the worth or the place of the individual within society as determined by his ability to produce goods and the second is that the worth or the place of the individual as determined by his state of health. The synagogue can do much to replace these false values with those which will help the individual preserve his sense of dignity and sense of worth regardless of age, productivity or health. It can do this through its educational program and through the pulpit.

The Jewish values which have particular relevance for the subject at hand are those which help the aging maintain their sense of wholeness and the members of their family a sense of community with them. Emphasis upon the performance of such commandments as the study of Torah, the pursuit of knowledge for its own sake, the dispensing of *Tzedakah,* the rendering of service may be helpful in guiding the aged to reconstruct their lives when former sources of strength have weakened. The necessity to accept responsibility (as emphasized in Bar Mitzvah and Confirmation), the link between the generations (as emphasized in the *v'ahavtah* and introductions to the *kaddish* in the *Union Prayer Book*) may be helpful in supporting the younger members of the family in their efforts to help the aged achieve a serene and dignified old age.

Bibliography

Allport, Gordon W. *The Individual and His Religion.* New York: The Macmillan Company, 1960.

Berezin, Martin A. and Cath, Stanley H. *Geriatric Psychiatry.* New York: International Universities Press, Inc., 1965.

Bowers, Margaretta K. *Counseling The Dying.* New York: Thomas Nelson and Sons, 1964.

Brown, J. Paul. *Counseling With Senior Citizens.* Englewood Cliffs, N. J.: Prentice-Hall, Inc., 1964.

Feifel, Herman. *The Meaning of Death.* New York: McGraw-Hill, 1959.

Moser, Leslie E. *Counseling: A Modern Emphasis in Religion.* Englewood Cliffs, N. J.: Prentice-Hall, Inc., 1962.

V

Israel J. Gerber

The Rabbi
and the
Mentally Ill

Preface

BEN looked sick, and he felt sick. Long visits in various doctors' offices and a thorough physical checkup at a world-famous clinic all pointed to a conclusion he found difficult to accept. There was no physical cause for his poor health. He was suffering a mental illness!

On the repeated advice to consult with a psychiatrist or his rabbi, or both, he had chosen first the rabbi. He feared that his wife and associates would think him crazy if he went to a psychiatrist. On the other hand, he expected little of the rabbi. What could *he* know of the confusion that had disordered his thoughts, poisoned his work, alienated his family, and weakened his entire physical being? Would the rabbi point a finger at him and ask, "Where have you been since last Yom Kippur?" If he did, Ben swore he would get up and walk out.

Ben was a Jew by birth and by association, but he knew little of his religion. He was afraid Judaism would heap guilt and blame on him or demand some rigamarole of atonement.

[63]

Still, he wanted desperately to regain control of himself and of his life. So it was with as much doubt as hope that he asked, "Rabbi, can you help me?"

The Problem

When an individual finds life unbearable—when the available choices are equally repugnant, when right is indistinguishable from wrong, and another day of life is as unwelcome as the day of death—then, and sometimes only then, will he seek the meaning of life. A person so disturbed wants to know, "Why has this happened to me?" Or if he thinks in religious terms, "Why has God forsaken me?" On the surface, these might seem rhetorical or academic questions. But when one experiences the disintegration of self, a mental breakdown, the questions reveal personal psychic wounds of the deepest magnitude. At such a time, the so-called rational explanations on suffering are without meaning. "A sigh resulting from anxiety," says the Talmud, "breaks in two the body of man."

All illness is meaningful. It expresses a conflict between the specific needs of the individual and his environment. When the friction between them exceeds the individual's frustration tolerance, disease begins. Healing means that a bearable relationship with his environment is restored.

Most people accept infections and other physical ailments as resulting from factors within the environment. Not many, however, view the symptoms of emotional illness in the same way. The more disabling an illness, the less inclined they are to admit that the change in their personality results from conflict with their environment.

Symptoms of Mental Illness

The symptoms of mental illness betray that the individual has a weak spot in his emotional make-up. By internalizing pathological social processes, he dramatizes his struggle with an insoluble problem: Impulses blocked in the past have now gathered force and are threatening to over power him. Mental breakdown is his way of telling the world that he bears a sense of personal failure, of guilt too intolerable for him to handle alone. It is his faulty way of approaching need fulfilment.

The troubled person generally suffers physical pain along with his mental pain, for mind and body are one. "A tranquil heart is the life of the flesh; but envy is the rottenness of the bones" (*Proverbs* 14:30). The Talmud also affirms that the body is influenced by thought (*Yoma* 29a). Since mind and body are inter-dependent, both, in the Midrash, are held accountable when a person commits a sin (*Tanhuma Vayikra* 11). As physical illness can affect the mind, mental disturbance can upset the orderly functioning of the physical organism. Probably the shortest and most graphic description is found in Proverbs: "A broken spirit drieth the bones" (17:22).

Medical doctors today estimate that a high percentage of their patients suffer from psychosomatic ills. About 50 percent of all hospital beds are filled by such patients. Most physicians accept the psychosomatic approach to many common medical problems, agreeing that gastro-intestinal disturbances, hypertension, asthma, allergies, migraine, colitis, ulcers, and many other ailments result from, or are aggravated by such psychological stress factors as fear or guilt.

Scripture recognized this long ago, as the writer has pointed out in an earlier work dealing with Job. And when the Psalmist exclaims: "There is no soundness in my flesh because of Thine indignation; Neither is there any health in my bones because of my sin" (*Psalms* 38:4), he describes the psychosomatic phenomenon. Apparently the author of *II Chronicles* also felt that King Asa's illness belonged in this category. He was critical of the king, who did not turn to the Lord but went instead "to the physicians" for help, complaining of his feet (16:12). The Chronicler disagreed with Asa's method, contending that the mind, correctly attuned, could have helped restore his health.

Psychosomatic symptoms indicate a loss of mastery over the environment. Prolonged unresolved conflict damages the integrative capacity of an individual's personality and thus weakens his ability to maneuver and resist the forces that threaten his existence. Faced with excessive inner and outer stimuli with which he cannot cope, he attempts, by means of psychosomatic symptoms, to re-establish at an infantile level his control over both his emotions and the environmental threat.

The illness that appears, regardless of its nature, satisfies his emotional need for attention and protection. At the same time, it provides a specific and, to his mind, acceptable focus for his anxiety. Obscured behind the smoke-screen of his physical complaints, the environmental threat is held at bay. Meanwhile, his illness dominates his relationships with other people. Since he is sick, everyone must accept his terms.

The peculiar nature of psychosomatic ills is that the patient defends his mental health on the battleground of character. He will say, "I know this attitude or activity makes me worse, but am I wrong to care?" Or, "I must do this," or "must not do that" because to do otherwise would reflect on his honor, dignity, loyalty, or faithfulness.

Conscience is the core of self-esteem. It indicates the degree of agreement between one's values and one's conduct. In a mature person, temporary anxiety caused by a gap between the two may be a sign of health, not illness. Mature conscience functions on the basis of what is happening now, not on what happened in the distant past. It is able to differentiate between adult and juvenile attitudes toward life. Otherwise, vestiges of infantile guilt continue to haunt the individual. No one who constantly is torn by conflicts with ethical self-esteem can enjoy whole or satisfying health.

Unlike felons, who are judged by society, the functionally ill judge themselves, but from a distorted basis. They lack integration, experiencing things that are out of context with how they perceive themselves. They are unable to reconcile their real selves with their conceived selves. To cope with their particular problem, some withdraw into a private world of mental isolation and indulge in extreme moral self-condemnation—the damnation of loneliness. Fear prevents them from sharing or participating in the happiness or love of other people. Others employ concealment devices to escape self-blame, overcompensating in the same way that a person with an inferiority complex becomes a bully or a shy individual becomes a performer.

The feeling of personal isolation—a striking phenomenon of mental illness—is often revealed in behavior that symbolically reveals a sense of guilt. Heightened awareness of unacceptable tendencies or desires may produce this guilt-ridden sense of isolation. Someone who bears unadmitted hostility toward others, for instance, feels unwelcome in their midst. Rather than admit his own antagonism, he will project onto others hostility toward himself; hence he avoids people and remains in isolation.

Whatever the cause of isolation, the emotionally disturbed person believes and frequently acts as though he is not an acceptable member of the community and family. Since much of his feeling is expressed in terms of "unworthiness" or "guilt feelings" or "feelings of being sinful," it is a religious problem, for this is the language of religion. When suffering from physical illness, many people become more aware of sin. They wonder what they might have done to "deserve" their suffering, and they cherish an increasing desire to feel human and divine forgiveness.

Whether hospitalized or not, people in these circumstances often desire to "set things straight" or "balance the books." For such people, Judaism—its religious symbols, its religious leaders—can have profound meaning. It provides a counterweight to balance their feelings of unworthiness. And it is these who, seeking a scale of justice that will not wholly condemn them, are most capable of recovering from mental illness.

What Is Mental Health?

The area of mental health is so broad that it is no simple matter to arrive at an understanding of the term. No rigid formula applies to every individual. Severe forms of mental disorder are easily recognized, but not the less obvious disturbances of the walking wounded. And who will say with absolute certainty under given circumstances that a person is actually ill? The medical doctor may define mental health as the absence of mental disease. Psychologists, however, often view mental health as the presence of certain psychological characteristics. All agree mental health cannot be prescribed like a balanced diet. It can, however, be protected, cultivated, and provided with a setting in which it may flourish.

The individual functions in two closely related fundamental areas—in his relationship with himself and with the world around him. A healthy relationship with oneself is a result of one's early relations with others. A correct perception of others and of their needs, a respect for their dignity, integrity, and worth become part of his healthy self-image. If he can accept others as equals, then he develops a greater respect for himself.

Thus, a person would be called mentally healthy when he understands himself and his motivations, drives and wishes, while recognizing his liabilities and assets. But a healthy self-image must also be a correct one. This is admittedly difficult. It may entail wide fluctuations that find the assets now outweighing the liabilities, and again the liabilities outweighing the assets. To be called mentally healthy, the individual should possess a stable sense of inner identity and live a life consistent with it. He is adjusted.

The adjusted person is one who is getting what he wants out of life without undue conflict. The most favorable type of mental integration is found in those individuals who strive to fulfil the highest needs of mankind and do so with a minimum of friction. He strives to develop his own capabilities within the social frame-work and to serve society, and derives happiness from both. Society reflects his mind and he reflects the needs of those around him. His willingness to take responsibility for his part of the social design signifies mature mental health.

In understanding mental integration Freud's well-known description is useful. He visualized the personality as incorporating distinct components: The id, which is the total of persistent, unconscious, infantile, pleasure-seeking and hostile strivings; the super-ego, which comprises the functions of conscience, ideals, self-criticism, and self-observation; and the ego, which is essentially the self, whose function it is to consider the individual's interest, to attempt to make his lot bearable, and to consider both the outside world and the individual's inner battlefield.

The ego can be seen as making compromises to effect a balance between the drives (id) and the restraints (superego), which are at cross purposes. A proper balance produces a healthy adjustment within the personality and society, while a rigid balance is unhealthy. The person who does not appear to respond to stress at all may go utterly to pieces after reaching an unbearable degree of stress. Where the balance is flexible or healthy, he will respond whenever adjustments are necessary. Mental health and illness are thus determined to a large extent by the responses or decisions made by the individual in specific relationships.

Criteria for healthy relations to the external world include the individual's autonomy—his ability to make decisions based on internalized standards rather than on expediency and the ease of implementing them. A person who lacks autonomy treads the path of least resistance. Then there is one's perception of the world, of external objects and events based on reality, not on wishful thinking or distortions of fact. Also, there are his efforts at mastering the environment, including his ability to adequately love, work, and play; his freedom to be reasonably aggressive in interpersonal relations; his flexibility in meeting unexpected situations; his efficiency in engaging in appropriate ways of problem solving, although not necessarily in arriving at solutions.

Absence of some or all of these capacities for adjustment may indicate a neurotic personality, an unstable and confused mind. When conscious attitudes and activities are motivated by unconscious forces, they are termed compulsive. In fact, neurotic and psychotic behavior are indications that unconscious needs have penetrated or overcome the controls of the conscious. Such behavior is often a defense against unacceptable unconscious drives. Not only the behavior, but the individual's emotional response to his compulsive behavior, constitute the symptoms from which judgments can be made concerning his mental health.

Mental Illness Among Jews

In the Bible, insanity is seldom mentioned. It tells of David's stratagem in Gath, where he feigned madness to avoid capture (*I Samuel* 21:15–16). King Achish felt he had more than his share of madmen already and was loathe to look at another. There is sufficient information to conclude that King Saul suffered a real emotional illness and Job an involutional melancholia.

In Biblical days there was a special dread of lunacy, because such people were regarded as possessed of supernatural powers. The ecstatic moods of the prophets and the behavior of the insane were often confused in the minds of the people. Since convulsions of the body were common to both, the ancients felt they were one and the same. Consequently, the insane were reverenced, as they still are, to a degree, in Eastern countries. When Elisha the Prophet said that Jehu was to be anointed king, Jehu called him "mad" (*II Kings* 9:11); and Jeremiah demanded officers in the Temple to put in stocks "every madman who makes himself a prophet" (29:26).

In other parts of the Bible, being driven *meshugah* or mad is a consequence of disobeying God's command that follows because the individual has viewed horrible sights (*Deuteronomy* 28:34). *Ecclesiastes* propounds that merriment and frivolity, in contrast to the serious mood, is senseless or "mad" (2:2). Other references to insanity are found in *Hosea* 9:7, *Isaiah* 44:25, and *Jeremiah* 25:16; 50:38, 51:7.

There is a dearth of information regarding the incidence of mental illness among the Jewish people in the past and in the present. From the meager information that does exist, it appears that among Jews today there is a lower rate of severe mental illness requiring hospitalization than among non-Jews. In 1950, the rate per 100,000 of the population was 74 for Jews, as compared to 102 for white non-Jews. When hospitalization was required, most Jews favored private hospitals over public ones. For these reasons the Jewish people have the lowest patient load ratio in public mental institutions.

Yet, Jews outnumber other religious groups in seeking psychotherapists and show the highest rate for out-patient clinical care. Some psychiatrists believe that Jews generally are more neurotic or anxiety-ridden than non-Jews.

Jewish people, however, seem to have a control mechanism which sets limits for them. Some sort of impairment-limiting factor seems to counteract or contain the more extreme pathogenic life stresses during childhood. Throughout their troubled history their anxiety may have functioned protectively, immunizing their children against the potentially disabling morbidity often induced by severe pressures and traumas of existence. The relative immunity of Jews to such self-impairing reactions as alcoholism and suicide have been confirmed repeatedly; it would not be inconsistent to assume that their historical anxiety has also relatively immunized Jews against mental illness. Conversely, with the decrease of anti-Semitism, which has fostered the cohesiveness of the Jewish people and their strong sense of identity, mental illness among Jews may be expected to increase.

In a study by Dr. Abraham A. Weinberg of the Israel Foundation for the Study of Adjustment Problems, it was found that mental disturbances appear to be more frequent among Jews in the Diaspora than in Israel. Writing in the *Israel Annals of Psychiatry,* he showed that religiosity and strong communal ties have accounted for the generally good mental health among religiously and communally oriented Jews. Dr. Weinberg concluded that Diaspora Jews develop the complexes of marginal people, or people who have ties with two or more interacting societies that are in some measure incompatible. Thus, the absence of strong feelings of belonging accounts for the higher incidence of mental illness in the Diaspora.

Observations show that Jews generally feel more at ease when they live in communities which they know intimately.

In the United States particularly, religion serves to strengthen the individual's sense of belonging. It facilitates his accommodation to the culture of the majority while it binds him to the Jewish people. Thus, the study indicates a greater psychological need than many will admit for religiosity and Jewish ethical values both in Israel and the Diaspora.

Judaism and Mental Health

Ever directed toward achieving and maintaining the emotional stability of its adherents, Judaism is a prescription for living that helps preserve mental health. This is not generally conceded by Christian leadership nor by psychologists and psychiatrists who, being insufficiently educated in Judaism, fail to recognize its compatibility with mental health. In labeling Judaism legalistic, law centered rather than people centered, they fail to recognize that the purpose of law is not to impose severe burdens on the people, but to reduce friction among them and to promote the good life. "Great peace have they who love Thy law" says the Psalmist (119:165). *Leviticus* (18:5), the earliest book of Jewish law says that a man "shall live by them" and the rabbis add, "and not die by them" (*Yoma* 85b). Even observance of the Sabbath, which is included in the Ten Commandments, may be abrogated to relieve pain *(Yoma* 84a), or to preserve life so that one may live "to observe many Sabbaths" (*Yoma* 85b). Jesus echoed the oral teaching of the sages before him who insisted, "The Sabbath has been given to you, not you to the Sabbath" (*Ibid.*).

As the Jew moves from place to place and through the centuries, new directives are added for one reason only: To enable him to feel in a new situation that he is living in consonance and not in conflict with God's commands. No Jewish law or ritual is more important than the well-being of the individual.

Christian pastoral psychologists are in error when they assert that Judaism is devoid of love, while Christianity is founded on love. "Thou shalt love thy neighbor as thyself", the second commandment in Christianity (*Matthew* 22:39; *Mark* 12:31), is taken verbatim from *Leviticus* 19:18, enriching Christianity but in no way diminishing Judaism. They also overlook the statement, "Thou shalt not hate thy brother in thy heart" (*Leviticus* 19:17). It is necessary to point out that the Jewish Bible has constantly stressed that man's relation with God should be one of love (*Deuteronomy* 10:12; 11:1, 13, 22; 19:9; 30:6, 16; *Joshua* 22:5; *Psalms* 18:2; 31:24; 69:37; 97:10; etc.).

The false impression that the Jewish concept of God is a wrathful, vengeful deity is widely accepted without regard for such statements as "Thou shalt love the Lord thy God" (*Deuteronomy* 6:5), and references to his "loving mercy" (*Micah* 6:8), "keeping mercy" (*Exodus* 34:7) and "shows mercy" (*Exodus* 33:19). The "fear" of God (*yirah*) refers not to dread or terror but rather to a respect and reverence for His power which is sometimes translated "awe."

Often omitted in psychological literature are traditional Jewish patterns that foster mental health. Having observed harmful repressions resulting from other religious doctrines, some psychologists and psychiatrists (including Jews!) attribute the same faults to Judaism. Actually, Judaism frowns upon total abstinence from sex, wine, song, dance, and the physical comforts. Even a *Nazir,* one who devoted himself to the Lord by means of a rigidly austere program, at the conclusion of his term of dedication, was to bring a sin offering (*Numbers* 6). Asceticism is no virtue, nor is wholesome indulgence the occasion for guilt. On the contrary, tradition holds that "man will be called to account in the hereafter for each enjoyment he declined here without sufficient cause" (Talmud J: *Kiddushin* 4:12). Furthermore, "He who denies himself a good life in this world is an ingrate, showing contempt for the King's bounties and grace" (*Seder Eliyahu Rabbah* 15).

Jewish laymen, particularly those highly educated only in secular fields, also tend to ascribe to Judaism doctrines that are nowhere to be found in Jewish tradition, but which they have absorbed from the dominant religion and assume to be true of Judaism. At the same time, many positive contributions of Judaism have been appropriated by the daughter religion without acknowledging the source. It is imperative to bring attention to the value of Judaism in promoting mental health. It has all the potentiality of enabling man to attain greater self-affirmation and self-respect.

Judaism is not only a faith based on the reality of God and on the realities about man, but is a way of life for the individual and the Jewish group. It takes into full cognizance the dynamics of man's psyche. Rejected, compelled to live apart and subjected to every form of persecution, the Jewish people have maintained their collective sanity through the belief in One God. Since God is man's Creator, man is organically related to the Eternal, the Source of life. And since One God created all, then Jews can feel that all men are brothers, albeit their persecutors are brothers who err. As a result of the vicissitudes encountered during their existence, they developed ideas and ideals that foster mental health. Experience in dealing with desperately real personal and group difficulties taught them that it is far healthier to accept and to cope with reality than to attempt an escape from the conditions of life.

As a consequence, one of the most positive elements in Judaism is the manner in which it treats the emotions. From the earliest times, Judaism has granted man his emotions. It respects all dimensions of the human personality. The spirit is valued, but so is the flesh. Man is but a "little lower than the angels." Neither evil nor good, emotions are morally neutral, a necessary part of human nature. Even negative emotions are seen as serving a vital function. The Bible abounds with stories of fear in the face of danger, anger aroused by injustice, or guilt for having hurt someone. These and other emotions generally considered negative actually help people over difficult moments. Judaism has always accepted the emotional dimension of human personality.

In Judaism the real issue concerning the emotions is what we do with them. We can control them to keep them in balance. But when control is so complete that the emotion is masked or hidden, unhealthy distortions occur in our thoughts. Or, when we are shocked by the force or the nature of our own emotions, we may excuse them by blaming others or invent an evasion of the truth. Cain, for instance, blamed God for his murder of Abel arguing that if He had not created "the evil inclination" he would not have killed his brother (*Midrash Tanhuma, Bereshith* 9). Job, too, attempted to exonerate mankind from the responsibility of sin by blaming the Lord (*Baba Bathra* 16a). The Israelites also rejected the Prophet Isaiah's summons to repentance by attributing their continued sinfulness to the Almighty (*Sanhedrin* 105a). In each instance, however, the argument was rejected and the advocate reproached. Judaism teaches a better way to keep our emotions in balance: Admit what you feel, and convert it into something useful—*mitzvot* (good deeds).

In Judaism, man is held responsible for his own actions because it is within his power to overcome temptation. "Who is strong?" ask the rabbis. "He who subdues his evil inclination" (*Aboth* 4:1). Judaism recognizes that everyone is subject to sin (*I Kings* 8:46; *Ecclesiastes* 7:20). Yet, although man is born with a disposition to evil (*Genesis* 6:5; 8:21), he can "rule over it" (*Genesis* 4:7). Thus Judaism accepts man as a creature with both good and bad impulses, whose unconscious contains base and holy desires. It insists upon a realistic view of the world, life, and human nature. Judaism does not feel that it detracts from man's stature to admit that he is faulty.

Man possesses a *yetzer harah* (an evil inclination) and a *yetzer hatov* (a good inclination.) The *yetzer* refers to the force which helps form the inner man, to the thoughts and desires that are characteristic of human nature (*I Chronicles* 28:9). In Hebrew literature, more space is devoted to the evil inclination than the good. In fact, the good inclination is not mentioned in the Bible. Its existence in every person, however, was accepted by the rabbis and they admonished "Always incite the good inclination against the evil inclination." (*Berakoth* 5a).

The rabbis realized that "the evil inclination" is a subjective force which is not altogether evil. It derives its nature from

the uses to which man puts it. It can be used for negative or
destructive deeds, but it can also be used in positive, creative
ways. If a scholar, jealous of another scholar's achievements,
slanders him, his jealousy is evil; if, because of his jealousy,
he makes a greater effort and exceeds him, then he has turned
his evil inclination to good. The Talmud teaches, "But for
the evil desire (in this case, lust) no man would build a
house, marry, and beget children" (*Genesis Rabbah, Bereshith*
9:7). The Jewish people regard sex as a significant gift of
God and include sex relations among the wife's marital rights.
Thus, sex is not evil, but necessary for the preservation of
man. In fact, one rabbi believed that when the Lord said,
"Behold it was very good" (*Genesis* 1:31), "it" referred to "the
evil inclination" (*Genesis Rabbah, Bereshith* 9:7). Only un-
bridled sexuality, in view of its consequences, is evil.

Man is to love God with both his inclinations (*Berakoth*
54a), implying that man has it within his power to convert
the evil inclination into a force for good. Instead of destroying it, man is to make an ally of it (*Avos d'Reb Noson* 16).

The rabbis maintain that "the evil inclination" is present at
birth but that "the good inclination" is 13 years younger
(*Koheleth Rabbah* 4:9; *Avos d'Reb Noson* 16), blossoming
when the age of innocence ends and the age of understanding
begins. Bar Mitzvah marks the assumption of personal responsibility for converting "the evil inclination" to the good.
The study of Torah, the youth is advised, is the most effective
way to combat "the evil inclination" (*Baba Bathra* 16a; *Kiddushin* 30b). Centuries later, converting a primary impulse
into socially and culturally acceptable activity was named sub-
limation.

Hebrew literature also regards guilt as operating on two
levels. Inhibiting desire causes conflict, which could engender
mental illness. Experience teaches that eliminating all frustration is not the solution to this problem. When a certain
amount of guilt is kept alive over matters that count, it is
healthy. Judaism does just this. It aims to stir the conscience
against the practice of evil of all kinds. Thus, there is normal

guilt and neurotic guilt. The former arises out of conscious transgression of the moral law commensurate with the nature of the transgression. The individual feels guilty because he violated his conscience when fully aware. Neurotic or destructive guilt refers to feelings of guilt which have grown out of proportion to the transgression committed. The rabbi aims to convert the latter to the former, to help the person accept a measure of guilt, and change for the better. Guilt, therefore, like "the evil inclination," can have a beneficial and elevating effect.

God has given man the gift of free will—the opportunity to choose between right and wrong. Man is both potentially creative and potentially destructive. He can either retain the birthright or sell it; enter the promised land or wander in the wilderness. The door is open for him to walk along the road of his choice (*Makkoth* 10b). And, in whichever direction he chooses to walk, assistance is given him (*Shabbath* 104a). But man must make the initial move.

To maintain that man and his works are subject to error or sin is not cynicism; it is to accept reality. Cynicism results from misplaced faith. When qualities of perfection are attributed to someone who proves to be less than perfect, shock follows. Since our belief helps to determine what we are, we need a workable faith before the fragments of life can fall into place. Faith does not free us from inner turmoil or guarantee that all problems will be solved. But Judaism helps us to see ourselves honestly and accept life as it is. We may not conquer the world, but neither will the world conquer us.

In the area of thought, the approach of Judaism is healthy. Realistically, it recognizes that man is never free from unwholesome thoughts (*Baba Bathra* 164b). But, says Judaism, let it not plague you. Although they may exclude one from the presence of God (*Niddah* 13b), unwholesome thoughts are not evil (*Kiddushin* 40a) unless they are expressed in action. Mere thought has no deleterious effect upon society. On the other hand, an unfulfilled good intention is regarded as though it has been accomplished (*Kiddushin* 40a). In fact, meditating repentance can wipe out an entire career of shameful behavior (*Kiddushin* 49b).

At times, the Bible is brutally frank in its descriptions of individuals and events. The first Jews, the progenitors of Israel and Judaism, do not appear as supermen and superwomen. Rather, they are depicted as living ordinary lives. They had their troubles, disappointments, quarrels. The Patriarchs, the Judges, the Prophets, the Kings—all are presented in human terms with their moments of weakness, discouragement, and even rebellion against the teachings of their faith.

Throughout, the authors of the Bible do not condemn the emotions. The feelings of the people are recorded freely and without judgment. They stress, however, that man's deeds— his good deeds—can best "the evil inclination." Piety is expressed by a concern for others, by just dealings with one's fellow man. In this tradition, Judaism holds that men are not to consider themselves sinful or be burdened by guilt because they have human weaknesses, depraved thoughts, and unwholesome impulses. They need to view their undesirable feelings, but not fear them. We may not be pleased with our emotions—we may even be ashamed of them—but we are not to blame or punish ourselves for what we feel, because it only compounds anxiety and weakens psychic strength. These emotions alter the functions of the mind and body and can drive one beyond his endurance.

But when it comes to our actions, we are wholly accountable. This thought is conveyed repeatedly in Biblical characterizations of Jewish heroes with their woeful human weaknesses. They were not saints, but men with noble aspirations. Accordingly, the rabbis teach that one hour of repentance and good deeds in this world is a more worthy goal than all the hereafter.

Judaism thus enables man to feel at home in the world. By asserting that man is fashioned in God's image, Judaism inspires man to confidence and belief in himself. Man has a degree of divinity within his being and, therefore, a propensity for good. Judaism has always pictured life as described in the story of Creation: "And the Lord saw all that He had made and behold it was very good." Man, therefore, does not have to deny or gloss over his evil inclination, but can accept himself as he was created by the Almighty. Thus releasing him from the contemplation of evil, Judaism elevates his morale and sets man free to act.

In the matter of mental health, Judaism's role is both preventive and curative. Health literally means soundness or wholeness. Through its ethical and moral teachings, its basic faith in the Almighty, Judaism aims to preserve one's wholeness or health. Far from creating a punishing conscience, Judaism attempts to circumscribe and fortify it. Jewish ethical and moral codes delineate the danger zone beyond which one trespasses at his peril. When ethical and moral values are denied or flouted, an outraged conscience may destroy a person's health; Judaism erects a guard rail against the hazard.

Judaism would define deviation from the norm, or sin, as a bad symptom (*Tanhuma Vayikra* 8). It denotes an unhealthy condition, that something needs attention if it is not to develop into a serious disorder. In Judaic terms, sin removes the individual from the presence of God (*Isaiah* 59:2; *Genesis Rabbah, Bereshith,* 19:9). It causes an alienation from the mainstream of life which not only affects the individual but has a pernicious effect on the world. But, says the Talmud, "a person does not commit a transgression unless a spirit of folly enters into him" (*Sotah* 3a). Evil is folly; the evil-doer a fool (*Berakoth* 5b; *Sanhedrin* 106a; *Sotah* 3a; *Avodah Zarah* 54b). The person who commits an immoral act has lost his reason and become dull-hearted (*Numbers Rabbah* 9:6; *Proverbs* 9:13, 16; *Yoma* 39a). It is thus a kind of madness or folly which strikes the evil-doer and produces in him mental and physical degeneracy.

In Judaism, faith is all encompassing and thus preserves wholeness or health. Man is the quintessence of the universe; all that God created is for the fulfilment of human life. The Biblical phrase, "You shall have dominion over them," establishes the Judaic concept that man's destiny, as William

Faulkner said, is not merely to "endure," but to "prevail."
He must go on, seeking and striving for the means of individual and social survival. Regardless of his station in life, man
can find fulfilment. These broad concepts give individual
man psychic space to grow in and time to conduct the experi-
ment of living. The good life is always ahead of us, attainable
in some indefinite future when the right combination of belief and action are found. Such a developing, growing, ongoing philosophy gives meaning to existence.

The Judaic concept of putting religious truths and convictions into practice is a potent factor that leads to growth and
emotional stability. To be really well-adjusted, one must resolve the question of his religious beliefs. A philosophy of life
that gives meaning to existence is of prime importance in at-
taining and maintaining mental health. This is not to say
that without religious faith one cannot possess mental health;
it is to say that the faith of Judaism promotes mental health.

Recent studies of psychoneurotic patients revealed that
their thinking about religion was confused and inconsistent—
which is not unexpected since their thinking generally tends
to confusion. What is noteworthy is that shallow and immature attitudes and concepts of a primitive and punitive God
were so frequently found among them. A large percentage of
their responses were concerned with punishment, and they
associated their failure in life with punishment for sin. Drs.
W. E. Reifsnyder and E. J. Campbell concluded that ideas of
a "strict" and punitive God and a "lowered self-evaluation"
exist in high correlation with a "subsequent narrowing of
life's spaces and proneness to emotional instability and social
maladjustment."

A mature concept of a benevolent God and training from
an early age in God's requirements of man are seen as vital to
the formation of a healthy personality and emotional stability.

It is characteristic of Judaism that the concepts of benevolence associated with God—love and justice—are taught as a
form of occupational therapy. One performs good deeds as
obligations to God and one's fellowman, and as a duty to

oneself. The Hebrew term, *osek b'mitzvot* means "to be occupied with good deeds."

The search for the truths that will ensure man's achievement of the good life Judaism calls study, and elevates its value to equal that of prayer. Each individual possesses a need to learn and to know—a need, paradoxically, that increases the more it is satisfied. This powerful impetus to personal development clearly places the Jewish emphasis on education among its health-preserving factors.

Recognizing that man finds fulfilment in his associations with people, Judaism discourages isolation. The Bible warns, "It is not good that man shall live alone." Even the lustre of the Garden of Eden pales when man has no one with whom to share it. Adam could achieve completeness only with someone, for a life alone is meaningless. "Do not separate thyself from the community" is another statement that reinforces this insight. Hillel thus expressed a basic assumption of Judaism that therapeutic value resides in group association. He foreshadowed the modern homily that once a banana leaves the bunch it is sure to get skinned. Congenial and constructive relationships with people are among life's most stabilizing forces. Jews do not feel alone, cut off, since they regard the whole universe as their home. The concept that God is the Father of all and that all men are therefore brothers to each other assures the Jew, regardless of the conditions under which he finds himself, that man is never alone. Judaism thus provides a sense of belonging and of togetherness.

For this reason, Judaism extols the value of family life as the cornerstone of society. The support the members of the family give each other enhances personal adjustment and promotes emotional health. Studies indicate that love is necessary to emotional and intellectual attainments. The individual who has experienced a healthy, loving environment is more secure, physically healthier, and has a higher estimate of himself. He feels important because he is important to his parents. His home serves as the fortress of his security and stability. His parents give him protection, guidance, and understanding. If the answer to mental health is prevention, then prevention begins in the home. Man's fulfilment, Judaism stresses, lies in his social existence. Mental health is everyone's problem. All lives are interdependent. All our destinies are interlocked and whatever happens to any one of us happens to the entire human race.

Contact with a group often entails fear, anxiety, jealousy, frustration, hostility, and a sense of inadequacy. These are the hazards one must face to escape the safer prison of solitude. To live a serene life, one should not enter business, or fall in love, or become a parent. Since hostility is a natural reaction toward those who frustrate our desires and ambitions, to learn to love and not to hate is man's ultimate achievement.

The Bible emphasized the negative and positive aspects of this great conflict: "Thou shalt not hate thy brother in thy heart." "Thou shalt not take vengeance, thou shalt not bear any grudge." But "thou shalt love thy neighbor as thyself." Judaism recognizes the value of love which defines the quality of a relationship within one's self and between oneself and others. Love promotes a closeness, a union with another; it binds loved ones together, affirming each person's worth as an individual. It is a total response which influences the functioning of the organism toward wholeness, while hostility and hate are obstacles to love and wholeness.

The problem with the mentally ill is to remedy the ravages caused by the deprivation of love, affection, understanding, and support. Having been denied these essentials to human growth, the individual feels his self-esteem threatened. Unable to face this denial while experiencing hostile relations with others, illness is his only defense against further suffering. In loving, Judaism teaches, the individual becomes his true self. By discarding unwholesome feelings he restores his sense of rightness. This is equally true and operative in man's relationship to God—to be healthful, it must rest on the total response of love. Thus the command: "Thou shalt love the Lord thy God."

Since Judaism is not blind to man's limitations, it does not make impossible demands upon its adherents. It does not require the performance of special acts of propitiation or unnatural suppression of human instincts. Man is required only to introduce *k'dushah* (holiness) into the ordinary acts of life. When enhanced by the concept of holiness, the doing of these deeds is elevated. Man eats, but avoids gluttony; man reproduces, but does not pervert his sexuality; man works, but not without respite; man reflects upon the past, but he anticipates the future. Any activity necessary to survival may, in excess, become destructive; holiness is the rein that stops man from headlong flight into oblivion.

Acknowledging that man is capable of destructive acts or error, Judaism grants him the opportunity to assess his deed, repent for his error, and go on with living. But repentance, the psychic catharsis, must be reasonable and moderate. When asked why the confessional is recited in alphabetical order on Yom Kippur, a rabbi once replied, "So that man will know when to stop beating his breast." There is no end to error or sin, and no end to our awareness of error or sin, but there is an end to the alphabet.

In Judaism all of man's emotions are treated in the same moderate manner. The active, fiery man is admonished to curb his passion, while the scholar who sits passively with his books is abetted to seek out his wife. Mourning customs strictly limit one's preoccupation with grief, specifying degrees by which the bereaved return to society after periods of no longer than three days, then seven days, then thirty days, then eleven months. Excessive mourning, both in degree and duration, is forbidden. For the human organism to survive, violent emotions must be curtailed.

Judaism gives purpose to man's life by holding before him positive and satisfying aims. He is admonished to right whatever wrongs exist. It is not enough to be good; he must do good. Character without conduct it considered empty; faith without action, meaningless. His religiosity finds expression through a concern for others, but with limits.

Judaism combines idealism with realism. As in other aspects of living mentioned earlier, Judaism places the rein of holiness or moderation even on religious expression. It encourages al-

truism, but not at the expense of one's ego. Man is his brother's keeper, not his redeemer. To fulfil this duty he must preserve the integrity of his own personality as well as his brother's. "If I am not for myself who is for me?" Hillel pondered.
"But if I am only for myself, what am I?" As Cain's question
yielded the inescapable definition of responsibilty to others,
the answer to Hillel's dilemma defines a healthy individualism.

Above all, Judaism is a religion of compassion. The Jew is
to bless God "for evil as well as for good," for life is composed
of both. To accept this is to cushion the daily emotional
shocks so that adversity does not paralyze one into inaction.
He must try to shape the course of his life, to help himself
through individual effort. If he does not succeed, then he is
not to brood over his failures, for man is not omnipotent and
must accept failure.

Even for the ultimate failure, the suicide, there is compassion in Judaism. Although tradition theoretically excludes a
suicide from burial in the Jewish cemetery, it serves more as
deterrent. Since the rabbis maintain that no one commits suicide unless he is mentally ill, the suicide usually is not denied
a sanctified burial. From birth until death Judaism is equally
concerned with the individual's physical and mental health.
It prescribes conditions conducive to both and is compassion-
ate toward those who are ill. In this vein the Talmud decrees
that if one's wife becomes insane, the husband is not permitted to divorce her because she would be unprotected and
would thus be prey to serious moral and physical danger
(*Yebamoth* 110b; 112b). For the protection of one who becomes mad, and in this state sells his property, the sale is not
valid (*Kethuboth* 20a). Furthermore, should a man become
insane, the *Beth Din* or court takes possession of his estate
and provides clothing and other things for his wife and children. One of the "other things" is cosmetics. This is done because it is assumed that he wants his wife and family to be
properly provided for (*Kethuboth* 48a). At the same time,
under these circumstances, the court can warn the wife about
being suspect of infidelity (*Sotah* 24a).

Judaism is a non-dogmatic faith with no formal creed. Consequently, it is compatible with the newest scientific findings and harmonious with the philosophies of the day. Judaism maintains that prayers that go counter to natural law or that which has already happened are futile and improper. In other words, Jewish prayer and ritual are not intended to control external forces, but are designed to develop and refine inner man. The Bible credits prayer with prolonging the life of King Hezekiah when death was imminent (*Isaiah* 38:1-5). Judaism claims no monopoly on salvation, but is all-inclusive: All the righteous have a portion in the hereafter. This is achieved through conduct, not by meditation, for the individual is God's partner in the never ending process of creation. Judaism's attitude toward life is optimistic and it demands full enjoyment of life for "a merry heart is a good medicine" (*Proverbs* 17:22). It is neither fatalistic nor pacifistic. To make the Messianic Age a reality, one can and must strive to eradicate evil, for it is hazardous to live in a world without all-encompassing values.

Although Jewish theology, ethics, and morality do not completely eliminate mental illness among Jews, the wholesomeness of Judaism remains unassailable. If mental illness befalls the Jew, it is not the result of unhealthy ideals, only that of human failure to achieve them. Some individuals reach higher levels of feeling, knowing, and doing than others, but perfection must forever remain an ideal; and psychic injuries sustained on the climb, the price of our humanity.

The Rabbi as Counselor

Since neuroses actually abound among Jews today, a heavy responsibility falls upon the rabbi "to bind up the broken hearted" (*Isaiah* 61:1). The rabbi has a definite task to perform and can minister helpfully to the mentally ill.

As the spiritual guide of his synagogue, all his activities are directed to the spiritual welfare of his congregants and to humanity as a whole. He conveys religious teaching by encounters with the membership individually and en masse. Almost everything the rabbi does has a bearing on his role as counselor.

The rabbi meets people beset with problems everywhere—in his study, at home, in the synagogue, in the hospitals, and on the streets. Resolving fears, anxieties, and tensions that develop from interpersonal relations at home and outside are within the rabbi's province. He ministers in face-to-face situations and from the pulpit. Sermonizing may be regarded as group spiritual guidance, yet it is offered to every individual present. Many will say, "I felt that you were talking right to me," and this may lead to their coming to him for individual consultation. If he is well-trained in the fundamentals of psychology, he is the congregation's strongest asset for mental health.

The modern rabbi's functions and duties have changed from those of his counterpart in the past. While he must be equally erudite in the customs and literature of his people, he must also know the current general culture in which the Jew is immersed as well as the latest findings and techniques of psychology. Because of the broader experiences encountered in the modern era, he needs a deeper understanding of human relationships.

A general knowledge of psychology and therapeutic technique makes it possible for the clergyman to cooperate with psychiatric professionals. It enables him to understand his congregants in their various stages of treatment. It equips him to make appropriate statements and to relate in ways that are helpful to people who are disturbed. Properly trained, the rabbi can shape religious teachings and attitudes to meet the needs of the individual. Sometimes the rabbi can reach a person who is unable to respond to the doctor or psychiatrist. Even among those who are most detached from religion, many regard him as having a spirit different from others. The rabbi should, therefore, never underestimate the religious feelings of those who seek his help. Recognizing this, the skillful rabbi can, at times, help a person transcend himself, face his trials with courage, and accept illness with greater equanimity. In such an instance the physician may feel inadequate, but the rabbi has much to offer.

The quarrel between religion and psychiatry has eased considerably. Religion has more in common with psychiatry than with any other branch in the medical field. Many psychiatrists would welcome a clergy informed in basic therapy and technique. They regard spiritual and moral values as essential to somatic and psychic health. Beyond the satisfaction of biological needs, they appreciate the spiritual need for meaning in human life. Courses in psychology and counseling techniques are in the curricula of almost all theological seminaries, and a host of books and journals emphasize the compatibility of religion and psychiatry.

With respect to Judaism, there is no disharmony between the two disciplines. Both Judaism and psychiatry are founded upon the dynamic growth and fulfilment of the individual within society. To this end, Judaism proposes a set of values; to the same end, psychiatry advocates adjustment. And what is adjustment if not the process of living up to a set of values? The well-trained rabbi understands the need for an ordered spiritual frame of reference for the mental health of his congregants, and he will encourage them to strengthen their spiritual resources. He certainly will not coerce them into specific religious practices, but will use psychological techniques to help them adjust.

The rabbi must learn to recognize mental disorders and develop the competence to cope with individuals who exhibit neuroticism. He must realize that pathological behavior is a symptom of disharmony between the individual and his environment. If he wishes to help in the healing process, he must be prepared to enter the turbulent atmosphere of the patient's world, without himself being swept into confusion.

Among those who come to the rabbi are people already receiving psychotherapy, those who are fearful of psychiatrists and psychologists and come to him instead, those who cannot afford to pay for treatment, and, of course, those who do not realize they need treatment. They are people pulled apart, lacking a unified, integrated ego, and suffering an inner conflict. They are seeking goals and a style of life which will enable them to gratify their needs. The rabbi deals continuously with people mentally disturbed to various degrees.

The rabbi helps them to discover the nature of their conflicts and to decide which of several conflicting desires they will subordinate to others. It is difficult for him to limit the people who come to him, yet his time is limited by his other duties. Any counseling he may do is an out-growth of the rabbi's love and concern for others, giving this relationship a spiritual dimension.

The extent to which the rabbi can help the patient depends largely upon one important factor—the absence of threat to the patient. Here the rabbi may have an advantage over some other clergymen in the role of counselor; he is a teacher of life, not an intermediary between man and God. The most successful therapist is the one who does not represent a threatening authority. And, if the therapist is one who has personally struggled and achieved an inner resolution, he is more capable of understanding the sufferer's anguish.

When he is concerned with others, the rabbi is participating in religious work. Pastoral counseling has traditionally been one of his functions.

Before the advent of psychiatry, people consulted the rabbi whenever they faced a problem of any dimension. They did not feel that their inadequacy meant they had to carry on the struggle alone, or that they should give up. Their rapport with their spiritual mentor helped them endure the period of stress. Despite the availability of other psychotherapists, the rabbi today should not be deterred from offering such help to his congregants as a member of the therapeutic team. Like other professional counselors, his aim is to restore lost, unhappy, and unproductive people to more meaningful, more useful, and more satisfying lives.

Unlike other professionals, such as the medical doctor, the psychiatrist, and the social worker, the rabbi is never outside his field when a person is in difficulty. Throughout, his role is that of spiritual physician. His duty is to minister under all circumstances; his profession knows no boundaries. In the view of Judaism, religion has a bearing on every area of human endeavor and relationship—in the market place and at home, within the person and among persons.

Evidence of the essential counseling relationship between the rabbi and his congregant is found throughout Jewish literature. As a result of many encounters, the rabbis drew up guidelines for their behavior when persons beset with problems called upon them for help. One rabbi wrote, "An impatient man cannot teach." A very good example of this is the great and gentle Hillel. When a pagan asked him to tell all there is to know about Judaism while he stood on one foot, Hillel did not drive him out in anger, but calmly replied, "What is hateful unto thee do not do to thy neighbor. This is the whole law; all the rest is commentary. Now go and study." To guide people, especially those who are distressed, the rabbi must be patient. He must be ready to listen, to permit his caller to unburden pent-up anxiety, and thus prepare himself to make a necessary decision.

"Receive every man with a cheerful countenance," another rabbi taught. This is regarded, he elaborated, as though he had given him all the good gifts in the world (*Avos d'Reb Noson* 13). Only when the rabbi has come to terms with his own insecurities and hostilities is he capable of helping others with emotional problems. He must cultivate the self-control and detachment that will enable him to welcome anyone affably.

One rabbi admonished, "Judge every man with an inclination in his favor." The counselor must not be judgmental in the negative sense; rather, he must exhibit a sympathetic acceptance of the person before him. To be critical is to reject, to infuse with a feeling of inherent guilt. In Judaism this is forbidden. Traditionally, the counselor-rabbi abhors any treatment that tends to degrade the human personality.

The rabbis not only provided positive instruction, but they also pointed out traps to avoid. "Beware," they taught, "of him who would counsel thee according to his own interests"—a warning equally clear to the giver and the receiver of advice. And, "Do not judge thy neighbor until thou art come into his place," which is another way of saying that man should not condemn himself. Under the same circumstances, the rabbi should ask, could he, or anyone, have done otherwise? The rabbi must know himself.

With the increasing, although still limited availability of psychotherapists, the rabbi in many localities is not the sole consultant. More often he is part of a therapeutic team which may include a medical doctor, a psychotherapist, family members, and others, depending upon whether or not the patient is hospitalized. Even in the presence of other professionals, however, the rabbi has a positive role to play.

Reassurance is most expected of the rabbi. Merely calling on a person is a real ministry. It reassures the patient that he is not forgotten, that he has a real identity. It tells him that the rabbi cares, that others care, that God cares. In this respect, the mentally ill are the most pastorally neglected of all synagogue members. They are usually not visited "there" because of distance, or because the rabbi feels inadequate and afraid of doing something wrong. A visit by the rabbi as soon as possible after the patient is institutionalized is a form of supportive pastoral therapy. It bolsters the individual's feelings of self-acceptance, well-being, and adequacy; it conveys an attitude of concern for him when he feels most estranged from himself and from others. And in the unfamiliar setting of a hospital, the rabbi is a link between the patient and the everyday world; his presence reminds him that life goes on in certain predictable ways despite his own anxiety and confusion. At all times, the rabbi's role is one of reconciliation—reconciling man to himself, to his neighbor, to God.

In terms of religious services, the mental hospital is quite different from the normal congregation or community. The normal synagogue is based mainly on the family unit. The congregation is composed of constituents who are bound together by ties of love, friendship, and a common ideal. In the hospital, however, the religious community is composed of individuals. Family ties and long term social relationships are non-existent.

Several types of ministrations are available to the rabbi when he calls upon people who are institutionalized. One thing that always elicits a favorable and appreciative response is bringing traditional foods that are associated with the different holidays. Also, ritual symbols are meaningful, such as prayerbooks, *talesim,* and *menorahs* for the Sabbath and Chanukah.

But most meaningful is a worship service. Joining with others is helpful in strengthening relationships. I have found that reading prayers aloud and singing in unison are therapeutic. A sermon which emphasizes God's love has an elevating effect and is greatly appreciated by the participants. Holding services with regularity also sustains and supports the patient while he works through his basic difficulties.

Just as a child attempts to find security and strength by emulating those who seem to him to possess these qualities, the emotionally ill compare themselves with individuals on the therapeutic team, adopt their patterns, and strive toward the standards they establish. Those who desire to help the mentally ill, therefore, must realize that patients are people, and people are more impressed by who the helping persons are, than by what they do and by what they say.

Communication with the mentally ill presents the rabbi with some special problems. When a person is so ill that he is out of touch with the environment, a simple exchange of ideas is virtually impossible. Yet a rabbi can have an impact even in such an extreme case, if he can bring the person to accept love. An actual experience will illustrate.

As a staff member, I visited a patient who could not be reached by the hospital doctors. I sat down next to him and said nothing for many minutes. After what seemed like an eternity, I asked, "Would you like me to offer a prayer?" He looked at me for a number of seconds, and then shook his head in the affirmative. I prayed. At its completion, he took my hand, squeezed it, thanked me, and asked that I return. The doctors told me later that this was the opening they had been seeking. The words of the prayer were mine, but the pa-

tient accepted them and this helped to set in motion his re-
cuperative powers. Prayer is an invaluable tool in maintaining mental health and helping to restore it.

Yet words may prove upsetting, working in reverse. The
rabbi should be able to convey an attitude to the patient
without relying solely on words.

By his personal example, the rabbi can make it apparent
that happiness and love are possibilities in the world; that
even if the struggle against his weakness often seems unbearable, it need not endure forever; that when fear is overcome,
life may be gratifying.

Training for Counseling

Although whoever gives supportive help to another is a
psychotherapist in the general sense, the rabbi does not auto-
matically become an effective one by acquiring an intellectual grasp of psychology. Mastering the theory without
developing an insight into human behavior, human motives,
and the causes of mental breakdown is insufficient. Too often
the theorist is utterly helpless when confronted by a real
client who carries within him all the subtle and complex defenses against anxiety. The rabbi, therefore, carries a moral
and ethical responsibility to prepare himself in the field of
interpersonal relations. He should strive for competence in
the techniques by which he can lead people with emotional
difficulties to recognize the causes lodged within themselves.

As a part of his training period, it is advisable for the rabbi
to consult a qualified psychotherapist. Neither a new idea,
nor one suggested by professional chauvinism, it is stated simply in the Talmud: "Correct thyself before thou correctest
others" (*Baba Metziah* 107b). To help others achieve opti-
mum self-fulfilment, the rabbi must first be in control of
himself. He cannot be all things to all people, but he must be
many things at the same time. He must be firm, yet flexible;
resolute, yet relenting. Although he hears all points of view,
he must lead—for that is his purpose. He must be sensitive to
cries for help and thick-skinned to ruthless criticism. He is

the voodoo figure in whom the lonely and frustrated stick their barbs to gain attention—an uncomfortable role which he must understand is a love substitute for the chronically unloved. He must parry all blows, bobbing and weaving rather than lashing out, and defend both his role and his integrity when necessary with a quick display of "social judo." The rabbi who knows himself can accept communication even in the form of an attack, and can respond to its meaning rather than the manner in which the message was delivered. The purpose of his relationship with his congregation is communication; the best way to keep the lines open is to reduce his emotional vulnerability.

In addition to the vulnerability to life's stresses that he shares with everyone, the rabbi is subject to heavy emotional demands in his ministry. In the course of a day, he may go from a Bar Mitzvah to the bedside of a person who is dying, or from a funeral to a wedding. In order to run the gamut of emotional extremes and remain stable enough to serve his people well under all these circumstances, he must be able to master his emotions.

The rabbi should, therefore, take a psychological inventory from time to time for his own well-being. Insight into the dynamics of his own early development and present stresses will help effect a change in his personal adjustment, if necessary, and improve his ability to separate his personal life from his professional life. And it will improve his abilty to handle his interpersonal relationships in general and those with his congregants in particular.

Upon analysis, the rabbi may find that he likes people who respond readily to his ministrations and that he is grateful to them for making his life and career more meaningful by heightening his self-esteem. On the other hand, he may realize that he dislikes those who respond negatively to his ministry, feeling that they cast doubts on his skill, usefulness, and purpose. Also, he may come to see how negative encounters with congregants have on occasion touched off his own unresolved anxiety.

A counselor's personal needs for security and satisfaction

should not interfere with his ability to communicate with a patient. He must be equally alert to language and the eloquent non-verbal communications of gesture, posture, expression, behavior sequence, and even silence. And the counselor must be stable and secure enough to consistently control what he conveys to the patient by word, tone, and gesture. To become enmeshed in his own anxieties is to be incompetent. It is impossible to over-emphasize the value of training to an understanding of mental illness and ways of helping people who are disturbed. Without entering into the comparative merits of various theories and methods of psychotherapy, training in any of them drains off the anxieties of the would-be therapist and enables him to work with the mentally ill.

Psychodynamics and Jewish Ritual

The rabbi encounters the mentally ill not only in hospitals, but in the course of his daily routine. Sometimes all that a person requires is the opportunity to talk. Catharsis is one method among many—as drugs, hypnosis, role playing, psychodrama—that helps achieve emotional release. Verbal expression helps to expel tension. This explains why therapists encourage their patients to express themselves freely. Not to be confused with therapy, catharsis is an adjunct to therapy. Permitting the patient to unburden his feelings is an entering wedge for treatment. It is a means of helping those who want to receive help. The rabbi listens, not mechanically, but with emotional detachment; he is always genuinely concerned, but is never personally involved. For some people, merely ventilating a problem reduces it to more manageable proportions; or a solution may tumble out along with the telling of details; or the patient may discover that what he is telling masks something else.

How important is ventilation when fear, frustration, and doubt build up psychic pressures that threaten violent eruption! Talking things over with someone not involved in the situation diffuses the emotional distress, provided the listener is friendly, understanding, and permissive. Isaiah described this role when he said, "The Lord God hath given me The tongue of them that are taught, That I should know how to sustain with words him that is weary" (50:4). In the Talmud there is a discussion between two rabbis analyzing this verse from *Proverbs:* "Care in the heart of a man boweth it down; But a good word maketh it glad" (12:25). One rabbi argues that the troubled person should talk about his problems to others (*Sotah* 42b; *Yoma* 75a; *Sanhedrin* 100b). He should not keep them to himself, but share his feelings with a sympathetic listener. Various other Biblical statements are in accord, such as, "He that covereth his transgressions shall not prosper; But whoso confesseth and forsaketh them shall obtain mercy" (*Proverbs* 28:13); and, "I said: 'I will make confession concerning my transgressions unto the Lord'—And Thou, Thou forgavest the iniquity of my sin" (*Psalms* 32:5). The corroding effect of repression is clear in this line from *Psalms:* "When I kept silence, my bones wore away Through my groaning all the day long" (32:3). Recovery results from facing the truth and honestly confessing it, and then deciding upon a new and constructive way of life.

Confession as an instrument of the healing process has been incorporated into Jewish ritual since the days of Moses and Aaron, and today it is an essential element in psychotherapy. A person feels safer, calmer, and less anxious if he can find a scapegoat for his troubles; but, since this diversion obscures the truth, both Judaism and psychiatry redirect his attention to himself. As each rationalization falls under close scrutiny, no one can blame his errors completely upon circumstances or on society. He must also reckon with himself. Confession is revealing oneself to oneself and to God. It involves a profound sense of honesty, a discovery of what is lodged within oneself that has never been acknowledged. To confess means to distinguish between real and imaginary evil; to confront our attitudes toward ourselves, toward others, and toward the Almighty. The patient may not be grateful at first for this kind of help, and indeed may become increasingly hostile the closer he comes to the truth he has so carefully concealed from himself.

In Temple days, when a person committed a transgression, he first brought a sacrifice, the hands were then laid upon it, and then the individual confessed "that wherein he hath sinned" (*Leviticus* 5:5). The reason for this procedure was to put the person seeking atonement in the proper frame of mind for the confessional. The rite itself did not absolve him of his sins. Rather, confession was obligatory. Also, in Solomon's prayer of dedication, he concluded with the confessional for himself and as an example for the people, assuring them that when they would confess their sins and pray, God would forgive them (*I Kings* 8:33–4, 35–6; *II Chronicles* 6:24–5). Verbalizing, talking about the actual sin, is still the most essential and characteristic element in Yom Kippur services as it is in psychotherapy. For the release from guilt to occur, then as today, the person suffering with guilt had to discharge the burden of his transgression in order to be reconciled with God.

But verbalizing is not the whole of confession in Judaism. Man is to repent; God does not repent for him. God does not effect a change in the individual; man does. When the individual consciously renounces and turns away from his unhealthy attitudes and harmful activities, repentance completes the confession. If he does not change his way, though he confesses, the Talmud says, it will "avail him nothing" (*Taanith* 16a). Neither is repentance achieved until the individual confronts the same temptation and withstands it. Furthermore, his sins against a fellow man are not remitted on Yom Kippur until he makes amends, or if this is no longer possible, gives charity to the poor instead (*Haggigah* 27a; *Menahoth* 97a). Charity is an antidote to sin (*Daniel* 4:24). Because repentance is the act of removing obstacles to future growth, it is the gateway to a fuller life. A man leaves behind his past activities together with the psychic burdens his behavior engendered and goes forth in peace with himself and with God.

Lest the analogy between confession and psychotherapy be carried too far, it must be understood that they are not synonymous. To consider them identical is to misunderstand both processes.

While confession is conscious, psychotherapy operates on a much deeper level. Psychotherapy utilizes various techniques that help the person reveal himself to his own consciousness; he becomes aware of determinants and derivatives of his daily conduct that he is unconsciously hiding from himself. It aims to elicit thoughts and feelings associated with the inner and outer experiences of everyday living of which the individual is unaware. It is a process of drawing out, of "forcing" the individual to remember rather than forget the past in order to bring about a greater awareness of what is taking place in the immediate present. In insisting upon remembering, psychotherapy advocates the Judaic principle "thou shalt not forget" (*Deuteronomy* 25:19).

Unlike the confessional, which deals mainly with the present, psychotherapy links the past with the present, helping the person to see how, and then to understand why, past patterns are operating in the present. It acquaints him with the hidden sources of his strength and weakness, which effectively dissipates unconscious conflicts and other hidden factors responsible for his personality difficulties. Psychotherapy is occupied with what goes on within one's self. It is not concerned with symptoms but with causes, regarding the latter as significant and integral parts of the total personality, and the former as superficial. While confession is extremely valuable, it may reveal only the conscious symptoms and must not be given greater credit than it merits.

Besides the confession of guilt associated with Rosh Hashanah and Yom Kippur, each Jewish holiday provides an outlet for certain basic feelings. Group culture necessarily inhibits the individual's free expression of his emotions, while ceremonies permit their expression in the group and at a specified time and place. Rituals may vary widely in different locales, but the particular mood of each holiday is similar wherever Jews observe it.

The Feast of Tabernacles, or Succot, is a time for expressing thankfulness in joyful dance and group ecstasy. A pastoral festival, it acknowledges man's dependence upon nature, and inspires confidence that the earth will continue to yield man's fundamental needs.

On Chanukah and Purim the Jew can give vent to his aggressive emotions. The anger, wrath and hostility that result from pressures in his own life can be sublimated and released against the ancient oppressors, draining off his unexpressed anxiety. On Chanukah, the Jew identifies with the heroic Maccabees; on Purim he eats the *hamantaschen,* symbol of Haman, and thereby divests all tyrants of the power to destroy him.

During Passover, the Jew relives the experience of redemption. Along with the children of the Exodus, he learns to pay a high price for personal freedom. If he will not submit to any form of slavery, the Jew must be prepared, first, to risk everything for his freedom; and, second, to govern himself, voluntarily relinquishing his unlimited freedom for higher values.

The ideals of charity and loyalty exemplified in the story of Ruth and reinforced by the discipline of living according to law are held up for him to emulate on Shavuot. Handing down the law to the next generation symbolizes for him the ever-continuing renewal of life.

Tisha b'Ab, the sad day commemorating the destruction of the first and second Temples, is an occasion for collective mourning. It makes universal the experience of personal loss, and demonstrates that one can overcome grief with resolution and courage.

And the Sabbath, a weekly reminder that man lives in the spirit as well as in the flesh, elevates his self-esteem. He cannot sink into continual degradation when on each seventh day he celebrates the holiness of life.

Apart from other values of the Sabbath and the holidays, the necessary preparation and participation in these rituals are forms of occupational therapy. The repetition of familiar acts gives him something definite to do. In part, at least, he knows what to expect. He can look ahead with hope to the end of a week, and beyond to the approach of a new season that will surely come, no matter how grim the present may be. The Jew finds assurance in the rhythmic regularity of the Hebrew calendar. He can face the future because it is not altogether uncharted.

Personal ceremonies in the life of the Jew also fortify his mental health. The Consecration ceremony, the Bar Mitzvah, and Confirmation make him aware of the stages of his development. They give him goals to strive for and they indicate to him as well as to the congregation how much he has progressed. He assumes greater responsibilities as he grows older, and meeting them helps him to mature.

The wedding, the *b'rith,* and the funeral complete the ceremonious cycle of the Jew's emotional life. They evoke feelings of commitment to others, hope of spiritual immortality, and resignation to the finite span of physical life.

The sages who gave form, symbolism, and meaning to the ceremonies and rituals of Judaism built an edifice that has withstood the hand of change. It is a home for the spirit of man, not a prison. Within its framework, the passions, the angers, and the dreams of man can live.

To Counsel or Not to Counsel

To recognize the mentally ill among the many people who come to him for help, the rabbi must be alert to certain telling characteristics. The mentally ill are unable to cope with their routine problems. They regard themselves as victims and failures, passively submitting to whatever comes along. Their will-power is shattered beyond their own ability to reestablish it. They have lost faith in themselves; their self-respect is damaged. They do not trust their own judgment and have few successes to which they can point with pride. Ashamed of their feelings, they feel isolated and seek acceptance. They are painfully unhappy and disillusioned with life.

Usually, when a person's attitudes are confused, his physical condition also suffers. If medical attention has not already been sought, the rabbi should encourage this precaution against further physical deterioration.

As one can understand, there are no guidelines by which a rabbi as therapist can select suitable patients. He is expected to treat all comers—an impossibility even for psychiatrists. Often his best therapy is referral. As soon as he determines that treatment is beyond his scope, he should bend his efforts toward helping the patient obtain psychiatric treatment.

In almost every counseling situation, transference is operative. Transference occurs when the patient reacts to the therapist as though he were someone else, regarding him as someone out of his past. He grafts onto the therapist the personality of the person who was involved with his repressions. Conflict with the therapist may be understood as strife with older parts of the self which have been shaped by experiences with father, mother, and siblings. A common occurence both in therapy and in everyday life, transference can function on a deep or superficial level. Hardly aware of the transference, the person knows the therapist reminds him of someone, but does not understand that he is reacting to the therapist as he did toward the earlier counterpart.

The basic value of transference is that it provides a relearning situation. If one's problems in adult life are related to a poor relationship with his father, relearning may take place with a father figure. The transference relationship provides the opportunity for acting out repressed feelings and impulses in a non-threatening atmosphere. One way of testing progress toward cure is the patient's increasing understanding of his relationship with his therapist. Step by step, as the twists of transference are worked through and a more appropriate image of self and therapist emerges, we may feel increasing confidence in the cure.

Since transference is a common by-product in the counseling process, the rabbi should guard against the dangers inherent in the transference relationship. In his case, transference is extremely likely because many regard him as a father figure. Romantic entanglements between clergymen and female congregants are not uncommon. Often, when a woman is seeking a security that only a father substitute can provide for her, she may get caught in a transference web with her clergyman. It is advisable, therefore, that the rabbi minimize the possibility of transference in counseling women. He should likewise discourage transference on the part of inverts.

The rabbi should also be aware that symptoms of mental illness may assume a religious guise. Repeated conversions from one faith to another may signify extreme insecurity or a continuous pattern of withdrawal from association with one's fellow man. Excessive religiosity may be a form of aggression through which an individual childishly attempts to dominate his world. Ritual is sometimes employed like magic to ward off evil, or to escape the necessity of thinking or doing. A child who extols the rabbi may be more interested in belittling his father. Another may insist on elaborate displays of piety in order to inconvenience his parents. Again, the rabbi may suspect neurosis when excessive love of God (or religion) masks an underlying hatred which he fears to express.

Whether or not referral is made, there is something the rabbi can offer at once—a warm interpersonal relationship. He can offer fellowship and the opportunity for catharsis. He can show that he wants to understand the person's problems and his feelings and that he will stand by him, whatever the cause or nature of the emotional upheaval.

If the individual is referred to a psychiatrist, the rabbi would still have a supportive role to play. Supportive therapy entails bolstering a person's courage over a period of time. It is a useful technique for the rabbi to use until the individual regains his balance. The patient may face the loss of income, a change in social status, the reaction of other people if he is institutionalized, and doubts concerning future employment. Anxiety makes him peculiarly susceptible to supportive therapy on the part of the rabbi. The spiritual leader and the religious resources he represents can reduce the patient's tensions, and help him accept his situation.

Dr. W. C. Menninger maintains that it is often helpful

merely to discuss the problem with a sympathetic individual —a trusted friend, a member of the family, a teacher, a clergyman, or a co-worker. Talking things over with someone not involved in the situation relieves those in emotional distress. A friendly and understanding sounding board prepares the way for favorable therapeutic results.

The Psychotherapeutic Process

The over-simplified outline of the dynamics of psychotherapy that follows is not intended as a "how to" manual, but only to suggest elements of the structured counseling relationship.

The first step in dealing with a mentally disturbed person is to establish a desirable pastoral relationship involving a dynamic give and take between them. Pastoral calls are of some therapeutic value, but for effective counseling to occur, the disturbed person must overcome his inertia and reach out for help by coming to the counselor. Here, on neutral ground, he will find that he has the rabbi's undivided attention for a fixed period of time. There will be no interruptions and the rabbi will concentrate on him. This setting gives the patient his first assurance of emotional support. The rabbi will withhold judgment on every issue, including matters of religious observance. He will listen quietly, calmly. He will not probe for information, but will accept with understanding whatever experiences and feelings the patient selects to reveal. He will, in short, attempt to see the world as the sick person sees it.

When the patient finds, contrary to his expectation, that he is neither criticized, nor lectured, nor smothered in condescension and sympathy, he may begin to feel that he can dare to be himself. Perhaps for the first time, he feels that he has a friend who accepts him as he is. These seemingly simple factors are essential if therapeutic results are to follow.

The next phase in the relationship finds the patient learning to reveal his problems, his conflicting drives, and his feelings about them. As the emotionally disturbed person finds someone listening and accepting his feelings, he is gradually able to listen to himself. He begins to receive communications from within himself—that he is angry, that he is frightened. He learns to listen to feelings which have seemed to him so terrible, so disorganizing, so bizarre, that they had been denied or repressed. This is a painful process —it hurts to wrench repressed feelings from obscurity.

If the patient finds that the therapist displays a consistent and unconditional positive regard for him and his feelings, he slowly assumes the same attitude toward himself. If his listener can accept him as he is, then he may accept himself as he is. This initial release from stress gives him confidence and enables him to move forward in the process of becoming. Thus, every therapeutic relationship is influenced by the character of the patient, the therapist, the environmental forces that impinge upon both of them, and the emotional communication between them.

In a good counseling relationship the desire to be honest and to be treated honestly grows steadily. The counselor, however, interferes with honest expression if his responses are directed to the content rather than to the feeling associated with the material brought to light. Inquiring what the person did or avoided doing may cause the patient to revert to defensive, concealing devices. How the patient feels about the content of his problems is the cause of his disturbance and the object of his search for wholeness. Responses that elicit expression of feeling are more effective in keeping the counseling process moving forward.

The matter of interpretation is crucial as expression unfolds. The counselor must listen intelligently for information pertinent to diagnosis and must encourage the patient to verbalize all he knows or can recall about the troublesome aspects of his life. An early diagnosis, however, is but a guide to the counselor, and should not immediately be given to the patient in the way that a medical doctor announces his findings and prescribes a cure.

Extensive experience with psychotherapy has demonstrated that confused minds may not be affected by intellectual explanation. It does not alter the basic personality structure. As an intellectual problem does not yield to emotionalism, neither does mental illness, rooted in the emotions, yield to intellectual explanation. Fundamental human problems arise in the area of personal needs and emotional relationships; they concern the basic satisfactions, fulfilments, and frustrations of living. Explaining too much and too soon hinders the patient's efforts to work through his own problems. When psychotherapy becomes an intellectual discussion or an attempt to teach or indoctrinate, the therapeutic process is blocked.

Repression is the process of deep forgetting; an experience is forgotten to the extent that the memory of it cannot be recovered. But, although the event cannot be remembered, it is capable of causing neurotic anxiety because it has not disappeared. Any unbearable incident may be repressed into the unconscious mind. And residing there, it engenders much distress.

When Freud taught the concept of repression, it was assumed that mainly sexual fantasies and experiences were barred from awareness. On the whole, however, people today are less inhibited and talk more freely about what used to be secretive and embarrassing, such as sex. Today, feelings of hostility, antagonism, and malevolence toward other people are more subject to disapproval in our society, and are therefore more repressed than other types of human experience and behavior.

Free association, an integral part of the original concept of psychoanalytic therapy, helps the therapist gain access to a patient's repressed and dissociated thoughts and feelings, which he in turn interprets to the patient. It is free, however, only in the sense that the patient is encouraged to express freely all thoughts, feelings, and fantasies as they occur during the psychoanalytic interview. Today it is regarded by many as a waste of time and dangerous. In some instances, as in borderline cases and psychotics, free association may induce or increase disintegrated thinking.

Another major pitfall of free association is that the therapist may fail to pay close enough attention to apparently inconsequential material and give a wrong interpretation. The patient's present interpersonal relations, which can uncover ego-defenses and the motivating anxiety behind them, may also be overlooked while the patient rummages through his past.

Some believe that more can be accomplished by eliciting the patient's feelings than by encouraging free association. This does not mean that free association should be discarded. While the therapist must be concerned with meaningful everyday material, he must not disregard significant historical data which the patient may intentionally withhold. It should certainly be used when particular areas are obscure to both patient and therapist or when a patient's flow of thought has run dry.

Other techniques provide the counselor with valuable information for psychotherapeutic purposes. He will encourage the patient to verbalize marginal thoughts that may arise amidst other topics, and to observe and describe physical sensations and symptoms and their timing. He may suggest literature which inspires the reader to seek a better life, portrays the love and forgiveness of God, expresses attitudes of resignation and faith, courage and action, or conveys hope that can make the present existence worthwhile.

New symptoms often appear during psychotherapy. They are really defenses against the release of expression. Most patients suffer feelings of anxiety and insecurity and feel profoundly the need for acceptance and prestige. To escape the former and to secure the latter they employ such safeguards as sudden shifts in thought, tone of voice, rate of speech, body tension or motor activity; show fatigue, embarrassment or the need to be plausible, perfect, or apologetic. Attention should be paid to the repetitional, the transference character of defensive symptoms, especially as they relate to others, including the therapist.

Patients use still other devices, such as silence or resistance to relevant communication. Resistance is outside the patient's awareness. He fears that collaborating with the therapist in interpreting his expression may reactivate the anxieties which he originally barred from awareness.

Partial relief from stress and release of expression still leave the mentally ill patient far from cured. Only when he can attribute correct meaning to his feelings does therapy and healing begin. Being mentally ill, however, he is incapable of doing interpretive work without assistance. Acting as catalyst, the therapist energizes the patient to explore his deeper psychic life and the effects of his past experience. With the repressed material threatening to erupt into consciousness, the patient anxiously avoids its recall because he fears reliving the pain or experiencing the greater anxiety it would arouse. Psychoanalysts agree that this is one cause of psychopathological development. Yet interpretive recall is an integral part of therapy.

When the therapist offers an interpretation, he is making the patient aware of what he had communicated earlier without having been conscious of its content, dynamics, or connection with past or present experiences or emotions. Just how the therapist does this, and when, are key factors in the success or failure of therapy. For "A word fitly spoken is like apples of gold in settings of silver" (*Proverbs* 25:11). If his means of conveying an interpretation is wrong, or ill-timed, the therapist will encounter continued resistance from the patient. These resistive maneuvers should be pointed out to the patient when a good counseling relationship has been sufficiently established. The therapist should make certain, however, that the patient understands that his resistance is unintentional and that no reproach was intended; his resistance is only symptomatic. The counselor who is unprepared to recognize the countless subtle forms of resistance will be pulled in every direction without success. Some patients, of course, are not so subtle; they just never return.

Others may be afraid to accept the therapist's suggested interpretation because it may express acceptance of him. The mentally ill always fear the rebuke which may follow such acceptance and the reactions of hatred rebuke will engender in them. Some patients are afraid they may become obligated to the therapist by accepting anything beneficial from him.

Resistance in others takes the form of feigned deafness—they just don't hear the suggested interpretation. One may protest that he cannot concentrate any longer. Psychoneurotics may use selective inattention and distort what they are told; schizophrenics may withdraw into a hallucinatory realm; obsessional patients may use argumentation, repetition, and distractive trivia, or display rigid thinking to frustrate the therapist's attempts to interpret their anxieties and insecurity. Others become facetious, making fun of the therapist, or the therapeutic procedure, or himself as subject of the procedure. Changing the subject or bringing up somatic symptoms are also employed to draw the attention of the therapist away from the unwelcome interpretation of the problem. In severe cases, talking about the therapist may be the only way to overcome the initial reluctance to speak at all. Resistive silence, alleged inability to recall interpretations from a previous interview, missing scheduled appointments, attempts at evasiveness, flight into irrelevancies, a blank expression, marked glibness—all these indicate poor method and wrong timing in interpretation.

Before interpretation takes place, the therapist should feel confident that all pertinent information has been exposed and that the patient is sufficiently integrated to handle the anxiety which may be temporarily aroused. The therapist must understand that interpretations will denude the patient of his previous defenses against the anxiety. Interpretations should wait, therefore, until the counselor has an over-all diagnostic picture of the personality and the basic psychopathology of the patient. Timing must be left to the experience and intuition of the therapist. When the therapist knows approximately with whom he is dealing, he should be ready to approach the patient with therapeutic techniques. If, at this point, the relationship between the therapist and the patient is predominantly friendly, the chances of their acceptance are good.

It is best, as a rule, not to offer interpretations directly but to elicit interpretive responses when the patient has reached a point bordering upon an awareness of the problem. When the patient spontaneously discovers for himself the meaning that has heretofore eluded him, he will more readily accept the interpretation.

Sometimes, however, therapy comes to a stalemate because the patient is unable to step over the line from expression to interpretation. A "shot in the dark" may be needed to evoke some type of response. If the patient becomes upset or angry, it may indicate that the suggested interpretation is correct, or close. Often it is advisable to pursue the point. Some patients will partially agree with the therapist; they can accept interpretive suggestions intellectually, but not emotionally. These are the times when the therapist regrets a lack of patience and must follow the patient's lead.

In time, the patient expresses his feelings more accurately, and judges them less harshly. The less he suffers disharmony, inconsistency, incongruence, and confusion, the more he is able to accept himself. He finds it possible to abandon the façades that he has used, to drop his defensive behavior, and more openly be what he truly is.

As these changes occur, he becomes more self-aware, more self-acceptant, and less defensive. With a new and more accurate perception of himself, he sees his life from a new perspective. The landmarks of his relationships shift. What formerly loomed as threatening may be seen as benign, what had previously seemed desirable may become a matter of indifference—the old facts emerge in a new context. His life goals likewise appear in the new light of self-knowledge and the available choices take on more clearly delineated form. He finds himself free at last to change and grow in directions that will bring him more gratifying, and therefore more mature, satisfactions.

With this newly gained insight—a more realistic perception of himself and his problems—changes occur in his personality and attitudes. He becomes more like the person he wishes to be. He values himself more highly, is more expressive, more self-confident and self-directing. A better understanding of himself leads to greater acceptance of others, and he sees others as more like himself. Similar changes occur in his behavior, and his symptoms begin to disappear. He is less frustrated by stress, and recovers from stress more quickly. His everyday behavior becomes more mature and stable. He adapts to meet situations more effectively and solves problems more creatively.

It should be understood, however, that insight alone does not cause symptoms to disappear or neuroses to be cured. It does not initiate personality change; neurotic symptoms will not be surrendered because of it. Insight motivates the patient to move further into therapy, but will not do more, because to give up one's neurotic symptoms is to eliminate one's defenses against anxiety. In fact, if insights come too fast, they may cause anxiety. The patient will surrender his symptoms only when means are found to reduce his anxiety. This requires considerable planning and implementation beyond the dawn of insight.

The goal of counseling is thus not to solve the patient's problems but to help him achieve relief from stress and to gain the insight and independence necessary to solve life's problems as they arise. It is to help him modify his image of self, of others, and the related values so that the patient may learn the satisfaction of self-expression in consonance with the good in others, rather than in opposition to it. Its aim is to help him achieve self-approval through a reorganization of the self; it reduces the conflict surrounding his aims and desires, enabling him to become self-consistent and integrated; it brings his self-concept and his experiences into conformity; it helps him become what he conceives himself as being.

The foregoing description of psychotherapeutic counseling has been presented to give the rabbi or other clergyman a sufficient understanding of the process to play only a supportive role. The transition from the role of rabbi to the role of psychotherapist will not be considered, inasmuch as the reader has already been warned against undertaking counseling of the mentally ill without appropriate professional training.

When psychiatric treatment is less intensive or no longer required by his formerly disturbed congregant, the rabbi's role gradually shifts from supportive therapy to a service of reintegration and rehabilitation. At that time, his role often expands. There is a need for guidance in the family reorganization and in the difficult period of returning to society. The rabbi can help to create a social climate in which the patient and his family are comfortable. He must realize that it is worse than useless—actually harmful—to urge participation in synagogue activities if other members reject them. He will, therefore, refrain from discussing the patient with others but will demonstrate by his personal friendship and acceptance of the former patient that he has confidence in him.

The former patient, having acquired a better understanding of himself and some mastery of the weaknesses in his emotional make-up, is ready to grasp opportunities for a fuller and more productive existence. The rabbi should guide him toward participation in the particular facet of synagogue or community life that holds the greatest opportunity for service or self-expression and the least risk of failure. With skillful guidance and support, the recovered patient gradually turns outward in his interests. He becomes less self-centered and is stimulated to desire again a more wholesome relationship with people.

Counseling the Family

Families of the mentally ill represent to the rabbi vast opportunities for service, perhaps even more urgently needed than assistance to the mentally ill. While the mental patient is one person, the family members are more numerous. And whereas the shock is more intense within the immediate family circle, the ramifications reach beyond the family, affecting even people they will never see.

When the breadwinner cannot find or hold a job; when the wife and mother is estranged from her family and her relations with them are damaged; when the child cannot make friends or is having serious trouble with his school work—any one of these situations causes pain and suffering to all family members. Also involved are friends, business associates, teachers, clergymen, doctors, the police, and the staff of a mental health clinic or mental hospital. Directly or indirectly, society as a whole feels the effects of mental illness.

To serve the family effectively the rabbi must understand the nature of the illness and the kind and degree of the crisis in which the family finds itself. His work with the family is especially important because the attitude and behavior of the members of the family may aid or hinder the recovery of the mentally ill.

The rabbi can help the members of the family to maintain a more balanced home environment, and to cooperate fully in the patient's treatment by demonstrating an understanding, noncritical acceptance of the patient as a full member of the family circle. If the family is shown how its reaction may shape new attitudes, and engender socially acceptable conduct in the patient, the rehabilitation period may be shortened considerably.

Conflict causes progressive damage to the important relationships within the family, and prevents the returned mental patient from adapting to the home environment. Ideally, the role each member plays complements the roles of the others, assuring the mutual satisfaction of needs and providing avenues for the solution of conflict. Such an interrelatedness supports each one's self-image and provides a defense against anxiety. An impaired relationship undermines the emotional integration of all. A former patient, whose emotional stability may still be precarious, cannot be expected to cope with the many-sided conflicts of the entire family.

Since they feel that a stable home and family is one of the rabbi's major concerns, many families bring their conflicts to his attention. The rabbi should understand that some types of conflict are temporary and benign. They can promote the growth and maturation of each member and enrich their common experience. Malignant conflicts are intense and prolonged; and, because they are inadequately neutralized, engender progressive damage to individual adaptation and end in alienation. Despite conflict, whether healthy or pathogenic, family integration can be preserved through skillful counseling.

Because there are many overlapping levels of conflict, family therapy is an extremely painstaking and involved process. In principle, the therapist supplements the role enacted by each family member in relation to each other. He serves as a decoy, bringing into the open for examination the real nature of the various relationships. He often bears the brunt of the antagonism from all sides until the individuals perceive the need and the means for correcting their relationships. Family counseling ameliorates tensions which might induce mental breakdown, or which might prevent a recovery from mental illness. It is one of the rabbi's duties as spiritual leader and a vital adjunct to therapy.

Problems of the family must not be viewed solely from the standpoint of the sick member. Interpersonal relationships crumble as each individual reacts to the stress. Anxiety, the Talmud states, not only depresses the individual but also those in constant association with him. Strange and frightening behavior on the part of the sick one upsets them all; then, if he or she is hospitalized, the family must adjust to living without that member and they suffer reactions comparable to grief. Raw anxiety and depression settle over the household as each member sees his own dreams and security shattered. Each labors under a burden of guilt for his own shortcomings in the family—the most demanding of all human relationships—and when it weighs too heavily, shifts the blame to the others. Tenderness, compassion, and patience tend to disappear as each is enveloped in his own problems of adjustment. They need to know what kind of relationship ought to prevail with the patient, and they need help to respond constructively while he undergoes treatment.

Since emotional illness does not develop all at once, it is quite possible that the spouse was attracted to the sick mate to satisfy some abnormal need, a circumstance that may now render the spouse deeply disturbed and in need of help, though unaware of it. When the spouse does come to the rabbi for help, often it is with practical questions: How to help the patient, what to expect from treatment, what to do about the children, and so forth. Seldom does the spouse intend to talk about his or her own feelings, but rather maintains a façade of self-sufficiency.

It is most painful to admit the need for help. Lest there appear some weakness or dependency that may have contributed to the breakdown of the patient, the spouse may erect a defense against guilt. Because the sick one is so weak, this spouse must be strong. As the safety of a good counseling relationship permits some relaxation, this burdensome defense falls away. The spouse dares to come out of hiding and is then able to accept help. In order to strengthen and sustain the spouse and family of the mentally ill during prolonged periods of treatment, the rabbi must recognize and respect these feelings.

Sometimes the family faces a decision concerning commitment to a hospital or radical treatment. When a patient is so disturbed as to represent a danger to himself or others, he is incompetent to make such a decision, but frequently so is the family. Their judgment may be seriously distorted by the dread and revulsion commonly associated with mental illness. Feelings of shame and guilt, or fear of public knowledge, or even reluctance to assume great expense may persuade them to minimize the problem long after they have learned the truth about the patient.

The rabbi can be of help in such instances if he is adequately familiar with both the family and the proposed treatment, but he should never permit the family to seduce him into making decisions for them. Usurping responsibility interferes with their relationships and will remain an obstacle to readjustment. The rabbi must limit his role to support—listening, reiterating, keeping the issue open for further examination until an appropriate response is presented. Illness renders one more sensitive and frustrates everyone concerned. Frustration produces hostility, which in turn finds expression in aggression. Irrational resistance to the rabbi may then block his effectiveness in helping both the patient and the family.

In less acute situations, the rabbi should be aware that institutionalizing the patient is not always the answer, even though convenience might recommend such an arrangement to the family. If protracted, isolation deepens a failure in human relations and may further depress an already depressed patient. Drug therapy, psychotherapy, and the opportunity to replace malignant relationships with healing relationships may be what are needed for recovery.

Doctors generally look to the family for support and cooperation when a member is undergoing therapy. They provide useful information and may interpret the patient's past with greater objectivity than the patient. Relatives, however, are not always wholly dedicated to the patient's best interests. A doctor may find himself in opposition to the family on behalf of the patient and also on behalf of his professional integrity. A recovery may be the least hoped for outcome in a family bent upon exploiting a patient's illness, or his wealth, or who have other ulterior and unwholesome motives. Sometimes families are reluctant to have mental patients return home, especially when they had received radical treatment. The rabbi can serve as a buffer between the doctor and the family, rendering valuable help in safeguarding the patient's and doctor's interests.

Troubled people trying to solve their problems and discover themselves become overemphatically absorbed in the inward search for the real self, and thus to a very great extent turn away from the outer world. In counseling with them, any guidance the rabbi can offer in the direction of occupational therapy through service and good deeds will raise their self-esteem and have a stabilizing effect.

While it is important to know one's self, it is equally important to know the world in which one lives. One without the other cannot go very far. As an individual, the patient in therapy may improve greatly, but his social relations may in some respects be as lacking as before. He may be wiser, but sadder and lonelier. Individual psychotherapy may help the individual, but it may not ameliorate the pathology of a family relationship. It is not unusual to find that as one member of the family group gets better with individual treatment, another gets worse—the improvement of one becomes a threat to the other. This often occurs when only one member of the family is in therapy, or when husband and wife are in therapy with different therapists.

Individual therapy is not the only answer to the problems of mental health. When therapies are unrelated, the effects on the family are too often indirect and nonspecific. Helping one individual improve is not adequate therapy for family relationships or family groups.

In the minds of many people, the rabbi occupies a conceptualized role—he embodies the judgmental, prohibitive, and condemnatory aspects of society. He is regarded as the custodian of moral and spiritual laws. Since the patient and the family feel themselves socially isolated from the community and desperately alone, they may view the rabbi's visit as an attempt to pass judgment upon them. Such a response is often encountered among individuals with inadequate religious training. They usually have a similar opinion of the synagogue. It is important to help a person hostile to the rabbi realize his own responsibility for this situation; he is hostile precisely because he harbors ideas which are contradictory to religion's demands.

To overcome this type of hostility, the rabbi must be prepared to meet people on what they construe as secular grounds. As he demonstrates an understanding or a willingness to learn about matters of importance to them, his relevance to them increases and he sheds the judgmental aura with which they had invested him. Any area of honest agreement will modify their hostility and help them to see the rabbi as an individual personality who can accept them as they are. Upon such a permissive, personal foundation he can build their confidence in him and guide the family of a mental patient without directly involving them in religious matters. And, without really noticing, they will acquire a more realistic impression of what Judaism does, and does not, require of them.

Fortunately, anti-religious and anti-clerical bias does not

always obstruct a counseling relationship. More often families are familiar and responsive to rabbi and synagogue. They expect gestures of concern and would be disillusioned if assistance of some kind were not offered. (Indeed, those who are hostile may be still smarting over an earlier omission, real or fancied.) They know and long for the real living that others are enjoying while they stand aside, hip-deep in troubles. They want to break out of isolation and into society, but their anxieties and feelings of shame and inadequacy stand in the way. The rabbi must match whatever strength and ability he is able to discern in each individual with a corresponding need of the group and find a way to bring them together.

The Group

The beneficial effect of group association is gaining recognition today in all fields of behavioral studies. Human achievement in every activity from art to politics to the physical sciences reaches its zenith through the stimulation engendered in the group. More often than not differences within the group rather than agreement, set up a creative tension. Individuals frustrate and irritate each other, with the result that new solutions are found. Groups contribute to the physical survival of their individual members, and by means of positive and negative interaction unleash the dynamic drive toward self-realization.

Paradoxically, while social-relatedness is gaining more widespread understanding, a technological civilization is increasingly alienating man from himself. His feeling of self-estrangement grows as society becomes bewilderingly complex. Ours is the age of collectives—corporate business and industry, mass movements, mass communications. The individual is not counted; he is computed. How insignificant he is! How alone among the masses! And how powerful is the temptation to give up the struggle to prove his worth.

A notable characteristic of our mobile society is the weakening and disintegration of the family. For economic reasons, families are scattered and often rootless. Distant members can fly home, or make a long-distance telephone call, but the daily involvement in each other's lives is lost. Today, the aged are more numerous, thanks to medical science, and less useful, thanks to technology. From veneration, the old have fallen into contempt, for which they feel no less guilty than their children.

Competition in our culture pits man against man in the struggle for power, status, and security. His individual worth is measured by his influence, his possessions, and his ability to hold fast to these. Failing to reinforce his self-esteem in one arena, he will enter others where he again competes for power and position. Lonely, without affection and psychic support, the individual seeks companionship in organized groups.

But, multiple memberships are not the solution to man's inability to relate warmly and trustingly to others. Often members of these organizations suffer from a common weakness. Hatred of a particular group may unite them, or resistance to social or economic change, or nostalgia for a time that is past. Exclusiveness of one kind or another shuts out unwelcome reality. Or perhaps they all choose an absorbing game or a dangerous sport to escape from reality. Yet, within the group, they compete with each other for eminence or superiority, indulging in excesses that consume their time and energy and frequently imperil their health, if not their lives. Such fellowship only reinforces the weaknesses of the individual members. It is as if one non-swimmer joins hands in deep water with another. Or, as if one blind man confidently leads another over the precipice at reality's edge. Furthermore, the individual who escapes isolation in multiple memberships often finds these organizations in conflict with each other, and then he enters into conflict with himself.

Advanced communications are another anomaly in our culture. The more efficiently electronic devices transmit images, sounds, and symbols, the less effective is person-to-person communication. The script, the teleprompter, the commercial, propaganda, the staged news photograph, public relations, and advertising—these but suggest the hundreds of deceptions and manipulations to which we are subjected daily in our culture. In addition, heterogeneous populations lack a common fund of experience which alone can make symbols, such as words and rituals, meaningful and intelligible. So people ape the styles of an ever-passing parade of celebrities. They train themselves not to express their feelings and their preferences, but to affect a phony mode of behavior and conversation that will make them recognizable to each other. Their responses, therefore, are not their own, but a cautious attempt to surmise the other person's attitude. One selects an image and wears it, like a mask. Language, manners, all the subtle means by which we convey to other people what we are, are contrived to support that image. And since we are not totally unaware of our own masquerade, we tend to distrust what others communicate to us.

Tradition also fails us in a heterogeneous society. Problems that were dealt with in traditional modes and that went unquestioned in the closed societies of the past are being resolved today by conscious personal decision. The result has been a shift from a tradition-centered culture to a convention-centered culture. We look around us, first, to see how things are being done today. How people met this problem in the past is irrelevant, we protest. Times have changed! Instead of the time-honored custom, we usually follow the one honored by convention. Whatever the majority is doing, we will do. We are afraid to be different. So, we resolve our anxiety and insecurity by doing what the Joneses are doing, only to realize that conventionality stifles creativity no less than traditionalism.

Is emotional security, then, beyond our grasp in a complex modern society? Like everyone else, the Jew is affected by social change. He suffers loneliness and anxiety. He neither understands others nor is he understood. He resorts to both exclusiveness and escapism, he is a joiner of multiple organizations, he is conventional, and he is frequently neurotic, and, in increasing numbers, he is the victim of mental illness.

Stress can never be eliminated for the living. Nor would

man in a state of perfect equanimity be capable of survival, much less creativity. But stress can be mitigated and converted into creative, rather than destructive, energy in a suitably conceived group. The family, from the dawn of civilization to this day, remains the prototype for groups whose goal is the fulfilment of potential growth of each individual member. Even international government is described as "a family of nations."

On the personal level, the individual begins to function in groups when the family no longer satisfies his needs. Traditionally, the *minyan* serves the Jewish people as a secondary social unit. Ten men unite voluntarily for the purpose of community prayer. While each could worship alone, their interdependence is expressed in the required minimum of ten; each individual depends on the other nine, and the entire nine depend on the one. The individual's value is assured.

Beyond the *minyan,* the synagogue serves as a still larger social unit. Stemming from the core of a common heritage, the values of synagogue and family are identical, so that one who finds himself outside the steadying influence of family can turn to the synagogue for psychic support.

For some, the synagogue actually serves as a substitute for family. Lonely people find companionship there. A common faith and heritage promote a feeling of kinship with those who are stronger and more stable as well as with others who share their predicament. At a sensitive juncture in their lives, congregational life gives comfort, inspiration, and instruction in how "the family" has traditionally met their problems. Often this is just the needed boost to a drooping ego that enables a person to cope with his problems.

True, synagogue membership and participation are voluntary. Yet it is evident that the individual must surrender something to the group if the group is to serve him. There must be communication between them. Like a family the synagogue includes the very young and the very old, the dominant and the weak, the extrovert and the introvert, the philanthropist and the parasite, the gifted son and the dullard. Synagogue literally means "lead together." It leads together every type of person who needs something from the group, and everyone who has something to contribute—and no one can help being both. The speaker needs listeners, the teacher needs students, the actor needs an audience, the artist needs viewers; even the bully needs a victim. Each communicates what he is only as he relates to others.

Through sharing in the life experiences of the group, each achieves insights as to what he is, inspiration as to what he might become, and resolution to make the effort that community or group life demands. Self-centeredness is interrupted occasionally by unselfishness, and each individual becomes more social-minded. He is not only interested in what he can get from the group, but in what he can contribute to the welfare of the group. His maturity and personal worth are heightened. Synagogue, then, is no longer merely a word, or a name, or a designation for a particular building. It represents relationships with other people that have moved from the periphery of his life into significant aspects of his being. He knows others and is known by them; his presence is felt and he is missed when absent; he feels needed and finds certain needs satisfied there—all stabilizing effects and conducive to his mental health.

Above all, the synagogue gives formal expression to one's deep yearning for the Divine. The worship service provides a time, a place, and a form for the expression of feelings which are all but inexpressible—one's dependence, gratitude, and hope in God. Liturgical music, poetic and instructive readings from Torah, thought-provoking sermons, and the ritualized gestures of reverence for the Almighty Creator of the universe and life itself—all draw one's attention to the Divine and envelop him in a feeling of kinship with his Heavenly Father. Despite stylistic variations in different synagogues, the worship service does not vary with the changing moods of individuals; it offers one a support that is constant and certain.

The group life of the synagogue, through its ties with the past, suggests the future. While it enhances the growth potential of the individual, the synagogue simultaneously promotes the aims, aspirations, and survival of the group. The individual comes to feel that he can make the group stronger, that his creativity is needed to promote the welfare of the group now and to assure a future for his children as Jews. By identifying with the Jewish people before him and with those to come after him, he achieves a feeling of immortality in the future of the group. He comes to realize that it is meaningless to gain a knowledge of the whole Jewish world if he fails to achieve identification with it. Intellectual comprehension alone still leaves him alone and apart; to identify, he must invest in the future of the group. This insight into his value to the historical process of Jewish survival further bolsters his self-esteem and his understanding of the meaning of his life.

Although the synagogue is involved in the needs of its congregants as individuals and as a group—past, present and future—its vision is not only inward but outward. It directs the individual's attention in ever larger concentric circles from the self, to family, to group, to community, to nation, to mankind. The Jew is motivated to social action, intergroup communication, and philanthropic endeavors to open the doors to selfhood for those abused by society. He is challenged to become "a light unto the nations"—a living example of the highest purpose and achievement in human interrelatedness. His own fulfilment is incomplete without broadened perspectives and selfless action.

The synagogue, especially the liberal one, encourages spontaneous and creative new forms while it keeps one's eye trained on tradition. It aims to synthesize the past with the present. The individual's honest self-expression may take unprecedented form, but its roots are in Jewish experience.

In the general community, the individual's association with the synagogue becomes a frame of reference that establishes his personal identity in the minds of others. Securely moored in society, he can be honest with himself and with others, but he is not without a safety line that grows taut under stress and keeps him from becoming flotsam on the social seas.

Identification with the group helps neutralize his emotions and reduces his anxiety over excessive differences with non-Jews. It enables him to more adequately cope with the environment and fulfill himself.

Psychodynamics of the Group

The value of the group in promoting social adjustment and mental health is so widely accepted that group dynamics has become an academic discipline in its own right. Group education, group social work, and group therapy have all contributed insights that help define the group's stabilizing and therapeutic effect on the individual. Since group work is inherent in the synagogue, the rabbi is primarily a group leader and trainer of group leaders. An understanding of group dynamics, how individuals act out their roles within the group, helps him cope with the emotions of people with opposing needs.

Three principles underlie healthful group association. First, man is a social being—he has a need for others. Without association he cannot survive, for isolation leads to psychosis and the breakdown of adaptive capacity. Second, by striving for position and status within the group, the individual achieves the greatest degree of development and satisfaction attainable in the cultural context in which the group operates. Third, the group develops around common purposes, yet is flexible enough for continuous reorganization.

Every group retains some elements of the primary social unit, the family. The individual's first interrelated experience occurs in the family. His basic attitudes and personality patterns develop there and are carried over into other types of social relationship. Not unexpectedly, the groups that influence the individual most are those in which he spends the greater part of his life and upon which he is most dependent.

In relating to members of the group, the individual is involved in transference. Relationships in the earlier stages of his development are transferred to selected members of the group. The group leader or another dominant individual may be used to carry on an unfulfilled relationship with a parent; other members of the group may replace siblings. A more mature person may assume leadership, thus acting out a parental role himself.

Transference may be cathartic. An earlier relationship, which might have been arrested on an infantile level, now has the opportunity for fulfilment or to be outgrown. Because the leader and others may not react in the expected or desired manner, transference induces new concepts of the self and new attitudes toward others. Role clarification and correction ensue, and the individual is propelled toward greater maturity.

The effect of a group on its members depends upon the atmosphere or the quality of the interpersonal relations that exist within it. Mutual intergroup stimulation encourages a central emotion which, despite differences, unites the members in the essential purpose for which the group exists. Exposure to others heightens suggestibility and lowers resistance to new ideas and new insights, thus kindling a desire to learn and develop new interests. Furthermore, fellowship widens and corrects perceptions, while isolation establishes habitual responses and promotes eccentricity.

In order to be accepted, or to avoid extreme conflict, the healthy individual modifies his unsocial or antisocial behavior in the group. His emotions are neutralized when he assigns a higher priority to the accepted purpose of the group and to its shared goal. By discussing with the group the feelings which have made life difficult for him, he perceives that his feelings are not unique, but are shared by many. This reassuring discovery reduces his anxiety while group activity and self-expression drain off his troublesome emotions.

By participating in a socially approved and culturally significant medium, the marginal individual has an effective means of making his way back into group living. It enables him to find a place in the community where he had found it difficult to get along. In this way, the individual can be helped back to healthful relations with people. He can find strength and direction in this process.

When a person anchors his conduct in something as large,

substantial and super-individual as a group, he is able to stabilize his beliefs and himself against the day-by-day fluctuations of mood. The group lessens consciousness of self and reduces the emotional intensity aroused by concern with the self. The individual thus develops a sensitivity to the needs and feelings of others by identifying with them. Furthermore, by merging with the larger concept of the group, he assumes its central characteristics as part of himself.

A healthful identification with a group engenders meaning which gives our lives stability and continuity. A dynamic group defines for us the kind of person we should be and places pressures upon us to achieve its ideals. It gives us status and importance, opportunities for self-expression and growth, and an external standard by which to judge ourselves. It enables us to clarify our roles and to effect whatever modifications may be necessary.

Religious group activity should never lose sight of its central purpose to promote a creative fellowship for the healing and adjustment to life of its members. It is with design that the Bible places heavy emphasis on the relation of the individual to the group—to teach that only in human relationships does man find his identification with mankind and with God.

Conclusion

Our situation is that of imperfect man in an imperfect world—a predicament fraught with tension and stress. To live, man must press on to the outermost range of his ability to adapt. He must encounter his limitations and overcome them, or perish.

Whatever a person believes about life emerges as his basic philosophy and the pivot of his personality. If his philosophy and the activities by which he adapts to his environment are in consonance, his personality is integrated. This is good mental health, for man cannot live in opposition to his basic philosophy and remain emotionally well; it is also good religion.

Judaism—a combination of realism concerning man's imperfection and idealism concerning his perfectibility—offers an approach to living that fosters mental health. Jewish values reside in the individual, are nurtured in the family, the group, and the community, and are given fullest expression in those activities which achieve not only individual adaptation but which also secure mankind's grip on survival.

The rabbi in his ministry deals primarily with individuals engaged in the daily process of striving for self-fulfilment and social adjustment. Their tensions and stresses reveal that they are engaged in the dynamics of growth. They find themselves confronted by the dichotomy between what they are and what they ought to be. The rabbi should not regard as mentally ill every troubled person who needs his reassurance and redirection concerning religious values. Most congregants are not sick in this sense. His benefit to them rests on his ability to transmit to them the stabilizing and inspirational qualities of Judaism.

As much as his teaching, counseling, and religious leadership, the rabbi's personal example contributes to the mental health of his congregants. Mental illness and mental health are actually contagious. The person who is irrationally fearful, insecure, or hostile arouses the same or complementary feelings in others, with the result that group integration crumbles in much the same way that an epidemic destroys the health of a community. The rabbi should feel morally obliged, therefore, to fortify his religious erudition with an up-to-date understanding of interpersonal relationships and to confront and resolve his own emotional conflicts.

It must nevertheless be remembered that no man can venture beyond the limitations of his mind. Beyond the reach of his intellect, he must trust. Knowledge alone will not equip him to cope with life; nor will piety assure him resilience under stress. Noble principles, strong will power, a healthy conscience are valuable, but none of these are complete answers to every crisis.

Only the feeling that life is precious and living is worthwhile, that life can be a blessing, and that he is acceptable as a child of God can supplant despair with the willingness to live.

Such a faith accepts the limits of nature but does not presume to know what nature's limits are. Such a faith does not abrogate all reason, nor guarantee freedom from physical or mental suffering. Such a faith makes life an adventure into realms untouched by knowledge, and worth the risk.

Bibliography

Ackerman, N. W. *The Psychodynamics of Family Life,* New York: Basic Books, Inc., 1958.

Alexander, F. *Psychosomatic Medicine.* New York: W. W. Norton & Co., 1950.

Avos D'Reb Noson. Vilna, 1833.

Babylonian Talmud (16 vols.). Vilna: Rom, 1913.

Clausen, John A. and M. R. Yarrow. *The Impact of Mental Illness on the Family.* Journal of Social Issues, 11:3–64, 1955.

Fromm, Erich. *Psychoanalysis and Religion.* New Haven: Yale University Press, 1950.

Gerber, I. J. *The Psychology of the Suffering Mind.* New York: Jonathan David Co., 1951.

Goffman, Erving. *Asylums.* New York: Anchor Books, Doubleday and Co., 1961.

Hill, Reuben. *Families Under Stress.* New York: Harper, 1949.

Hollender, Marc H. *The Practice of Psychoanalytic Psychotherapy.* New York: Grune and Stratton, 1965.

Hollingshead, A. B. and F. C. Redlich. *Social Class and Mental Illness.* New York: John Wiley and Sons, 1958.

Jahode, Marie. *Current Concepts of Positive Mental Health.* New York: Basic Books, 1958.

Maslow, A. H. and B. Mittelmann. *Principles of Abnormal Psychology.* New York: Harper & Brothers, 1951.

Maves, Paul B., ed. *The Church and Mental Health.* New York: Charles Scribner's Sons, 1953.

McCann, Richard V. *The Churches and Mental Health.* New York: Basic Books, Inc., 1962.

Menninger, K. *Love Against Hate.* New York: Harcourt, Brace & Co., 1942.

Midrash Rabbah (2 vols.). Vilna: Rom, 1884.

Midrash Tanhuma. Warsaw: G. Piment, no date.

Moser, Leslie. *Counseling: A Modern Emphasis.* Englewood Cliffs: Prentice-Hall, Inc., 1962.

Oates, Wayne E. *Religious Factors in Mental Illness.* New York: Association Press, 1955.

Psychiatry and Religion: Some Steps Toward Mutual Understanding and Usefulness. New York: Group for the Advancement of Psychiatry, 1960.

Richardson, H. B. *Patients Have Families.* New York: Commonwealth Fund, 1945.

Rieff, Philip. *Freud: The Mind of the Moralist.* New York: Viking Press, 1959.

Rogers, Carl. *Counseling and Psychotherapy.* Boston: Houghton Mifflin Co., 1942.

Seder Eliyahu Rabbah.

Shulhan Aruch: Yoreh Deah (3 vols.). Vilna: Rom, 1894.

Srole, L., T. S. Langner, et al. *Mental Health in the Metropolis.* Volume 1. New York: McGraw-Hill, 1962.

Stern, Edith M. *Mental Illness: A Guide for the Family.* New York: Commonwealth Fund, 1945.

Talmud Yerushalmi. New York: Shulsinger Bros. 1948.

Tashman, Harry F. *Today's Neurotic Family.* New York University Press, 1957.

Toward Therapeutic Care. New York: Group for the Advancement of Psychiatry, n.d.

Ware, A. F. and G. L. Jones. *Ministering to Families of the Mentally Ill.* New York: The National Association for Mental Health, n.d.

Wiesbauer, Henry R. *Pastoral Help in Serious Mental Illness.* New York: The National Association for Mental Health, n.d.

Wise, Carroll. *Psychiatry and the Bible.* New York: Harper and Bros., 1956.

VI

Earl A. Grollman

Rabbinical
Counseling
and Suicide

I was a young rabbi recently graduated from theological school when I received this emergency telephone call. "Rabbi," the urgent voice spoke, "my wife has just killed herself."

I was shaken. I had already been confronted with death, mourning, bereavement. "But a suicide," I thought; "what do I do?" A hazy recollection of a Talmud class at the Hebrew Union College came into mind. Did the professor state that those who deliberately take their own lives are buried outside of the cemetery proper? Somehow, the entire incident seemed unreal. It just didn't happen, at least not to my co-religionists. So I thought. But it had happened, and to a woman truly dedicated to her family and community. I brought to this crisis situation my own existential anxieties and deep-seated prejudices against that dread word *suicide*. As a student, I had learned much about grief work, even about distorted mourning reactions. But for suicide and ministering to the anguished survivors—for this I was totally unprepared.

In the ensuing sixteen years of my rabbinate, I have received many such calls relative to both attempted and accomplished cases of suicide. I have since come to realize that the act knows no religious or creedal boundaries. I no longer regard it, as did some primitive people, as "a superstitious horror" nor do I subscribe to the view of some religionists, that it is a "sinful degradation." It is a tragedy—painful to contemplate, difficult to discuss, yet so real and pressing that it demands our attention.

I. *The Problem*

Once every minute, someone tries to kill himself with conscious intent. Sixty or seventy times each day these attempts succeed. Each year in the United States alone, some reported 25,000 persons take their own lives. Unquestionably, this number is even higher since the true cause of death is frequently masked. According to the late Gregory Zilboorg, Psychiatrist-in-Chief of the United Nations: "Statistical data on suicide as compiled today deserves little if any credence. All too many suicides are not reported as such." A police chief in a local town admitted that "If a man hangs himself, we just cut him down, rush the dead body to the hospital and enter some other malady as the cause of death. This way we spare the family the terrible disgrace."

The problem is worsening. Among people aged 15 to 50, suicide is the fifth leading cause of death. In one of the newest studies of suicide rates, the University of Michigan Medical Center reported that cases of suicide and attempted suicide seen by its emergency room staff rose 89% between 1957 and 1962.

Suicide which once ranked 22nd on the list of causes of death in the United States now rates tenth and in some states, sixth. Today, the toll is greater than the combined deaths from typhoid fever, dysentery, scarlet fever, diphtheria, whooping cough, meningococcal infections, infantile paralysis, measles, typhus, malaria, bronchitis, and rheumatic fever.

Dr. Joost Meerloo, author of *Suicide and Mass Suicide*, declares, "Eighty per cent of people admit to having 'played' with suicidal ideas."

The great medical statistician, Louis I. Dublin, recently told an audience of physicians in Los Angeles: "It would not be rash to estimate that perhaps as many as 2,000,000 individuals are now living in our country who have a history of at least one unsuccessful attempt at self-destruction. A great many of these will try again. On the basis of a recent study, 10 per cent will ultimately succeed. I emphasize this fact in order to impress the huge size of the problem with which we are involved and to focus attention on the need for a more concerted effort on the part of socially oriented groups to attack this problem seriously."

Dr. Alfred L. Moseley, who headed a Harvard Medical School team which recently concluded a careful study of automobile deaths, figures that suicides are a "significant though unknown" proportion of the 48,000 annual auto deaths in the United States.

No longer can the clergyman ignore the problem. *No single event carries so much emotional impact. No single event demands so much skill, understanding, empathy, and support as ministering to those bent on self-destruction or to the family who has experienced the loss of a loved one through self-inflicted death.*

Death by one's own hand is so terrible to contemplate in our culture that we tend to say the person was insane. Those left behind experience not only the pain of separation but also intense feelings of guilt, shame, and disillusionment. Anxious and grief stricken, they ask: "What will people think? If I had done my part, would this tragedy have occurred?" Death is always a robber but death by suicide brings about the greatest of all affronts to those members of the family who survive.

Society, too, reacts in a hostile way because the cohesiveness of the group is willfully and premeditatively disrupted. The manner in which one departs from life bears not only a positive relationship to his philosophy of life and death but a possible contempt for one's group as well. As Kant said:

"Suicide is an insult to humanity." From these taboos resulted the penalty of the suicide being buried at the crossroads as a token of disgrace and opprobrium.

But who is exempt from this "unpardonable sin of society?" Though we may never utter the word "suicide," does this mean that we are totally free of death wishes? From the standpoint of psychoanalytic literature, every person is a potential suicide. Every person has a tendency to self-murder which varies in degree of intensity from individual to individual and from one age to another. Bromberg and Schilder found the wish to die frequent in children, and suicidal fantasies common in normal adults. They concluded that the relationship between wishing oneself dead and a suicidal thought or attempt is quantitative rather than qualitative.

The child might think: "If I were to die now, would my parents feel sorry for their meanness." In chronic invalidism the patient often says: "My affliction is a living death. I would rather die than go on living this way." Or in desperation, the familiar words: "I just can't go on any longer," or "I am tired of life," or "My family would be better off without me." If these expressions repeated at one time or another seem unrelated to suicide, it must be emphasized that precisely these words are the verbal sentiments expressed by presuicidal communications and conversations.

In many cases where the person says: "I am tired of life," he may not play a direct role in his death (*mortus per se*). There are, however, multitudes of examples where the person in his latent wish to die may indirectly expedite his death by carelessness or imprudence. Unconsciously he no longer desires life and hastens his death either actively by a foolhardy deed or passively by failing to take proper care of himself. One may express sympathy: "Poor man—he lost all his will to live." But if he openly takes his life in one single act, we express horror and disdain.

The Suicide Prevention Center of Los Angeles has developed three workable psychological classifications for cause of death. An *unmeditated* death is one in which an individual plays no active role in his own demise. A *meditated* death is one in which an individual plays an active part in his own demise through deliberate or impulsive acts. Then there is the *submeditated* death in which the individual plays a partial, unconscious, covert, or indirect role in his own demise. Illustrations of the latter might include psychosomatic deaths (physical disease exacerbated by psychic factors that hasten death), deaths precipitated by negligence and carelessness (diabetics, alcoholics), "gambles" with death (daredevil feats, "Russian roulette"). Karl Menninger includes religious asceticism and martyrdom as effective methods of submeditated deaths. There are many ways of committing suicide other than by slashing one's wrists or swallowing poison, shooting or hanging oneself.

Suicide has been known in all times and committed by all manner of people—from Saul, Sappho, and Seneca to Virginia Woolf and James Forrestal. There is no need to create further fear and anxiety. But there is a need to remove the curtain of silence and with it some of the old fantasies and demonologic speculation associated with this taboo subject. We must honestly and sincerely view the problem in its totality. By removing the veneer, and by understanding some of the religio-socio-psychological factors involved in the taxonomy of suicide, we may prove worthy of ministering to the needs of our people in adversity as well as prosperity.

II. *Religious Concepts of Suicide*

A. JUDAISM

1. BIBLICAL

"And God saw all that He had made, and found it very good."

With almost the first word of *Genesis,* a thesis is stated that has echoed throughout the centuries. *Life is good.* Man should treasure it and never despair of its possibilities. For behind it is God.

Despite a religious emphasis upon the sanctity of life, the Hebrew Holy Scriptures contain but sporadic references to self-destruction. In virtually each case, extenuating circumstances are involved such as the fear of being taken captive or the possibility of suffering humiliation and unbearable pain.

The Biblical references are as follows:

Judges 9:53–54 "And a certain woman cast an upper millstone upon Abimelech's head and broke his skull. Then he called hastily unto the young man his armour-bearer and said unto him: 'Draw thy sword and kill me, that men say not of me: A woman slew him.' And his young man thrust him through and he died."

Abimelech lived about 1322 B.C.E. After his father's death, he murdered all his brethren. He then persuaded the Shechemites to elect him king. During the siege of Thebez, Abimelech was struck by a woman with the fragment of a millstone. Believing that death was near, he had his armour-bearer kill him rather than suffer the disgrace of being slain by a woman.

Judges 16:28–30 "And Samson called unto the Lord and said: 'O Lord God, remember me, I pray Thee, and strengthen me, I pray Thee, only this once, O God, that I may be this once avenged of the Philistines for my two eyes.' And Samson took fast hold of the two middle pillars upon which the house rested, and leaned upon them, the one with his right hand, and the other with his left. And Samson said: 'Let me die with the Philistines.' And he bent with all his might; and the house fell upon the lords, and upon all the people that were therein."

The story of Samson is popular with young and old alike. Samson, the son of Manoah of the tribe of Dan, lived about 1161 B.C.E. He is noted as a judge and as one endowed with supernatural power. While visiting a woman of Sorek, Delilah, he fell asleep and because he was shaven of his seven locks of hair was rendered impotent against the Philistines. A great festival in the Temple of Dagon celebrated the defeat of Samson who was now blinded and bound in brazen fetters. With the fervent prayer that God would strengthen him only this once, Samson bore with all his might upon the two pillars so that the house fell. "The dead which he slew at his death were more than they which he slew in his life." From this account, it would appear that Samson's suicide had the consent of God.

I Samuel 31:4–5 "Then said Saul to his armour-bearer: 'Draw thy sword and thrust me through therewith, lest these uncircumcised come and thrust me through and make a mock of me.' But his armour-bearer would not; for he was sore afraid. Therefore Saul took his sword and fell upon it. And when his armour-bearer saw that Saul was dead, he likewise fell upon his sword and died with him."

In *I Samuel* 31:4–5 we read of Saul, the first King of Israel, who lived about 1020 B.C.E. When wounded by the Philistines, Saul called upon his armour-bearer to slay him in order to prevent his being mocked and tortured by the enemy. Upon the refusal of the frightened man, Saul fell upon his own sword. In the next chapter, *II Samuel* 1:11, when David and his followers heard of the suicide, "they wailed, and wept, and fasted."

In *Flavius Josephus, Antiquities of the Jews,* Volume I, Book VI, Chapter IV, this suicide is condoned as a mark of courage: "And I have a good reason for such a discourse in the person of Saul, king of the Hebrews. For, although he knew what was coming upon him, and that he was to die immediately, by the prediction of the prophet, he determined not to flee from death, nor from love of life to betray his own people to the enemy, nor to bring disgrace on his royal dignity, but exposing himself as well as all his family and children to dangers, he thought it a noble thing to fall together with them, as he was fighting for his subjects, and that it was better that his sons should die thus, showing their courage, than to leave it uncertain what they would be afterwards, for instead of succession and posterity they gained commendation and a lasting name."

II Samuel 17:23 deals with the story of Ahithophel, a native of Southern Palestine, who was a privy counsellor of David. His counsel was regarded by David as animated by oracular wisdom. Ahithophel later joined the conspiracy of Absalom against David. It was probably the clear-sighted conviction that Absalom's cause was doomed to failure and that he would live only to die a traitor's death at David's hand which determined Ahithophel to take his own life. According to tradition, he died at the age of 33 years and in his testament he advised his descendants never to become loyal to the house of David. (*Sanhedrin* 10)

I Kings 16:18 "And it came to pass, when Zimri saw that the city was taken, that he went into the castle of the king's house and burnt the king's house over him with fire, and died."

Zimri was the fifth sovereign of the separate kingdom of Israel. He occupied the throne for the brief period of seven days in 889 B.C.E. Zimri slew the reigning king, Elah, and seized power. The army, however, chose Omri as king, who then marched against Tirzah, where Zimri was living. Zimri retreated into the innermost part of the castle, set it on fire and perished in the ruins. Suicide was provoked for fear of the foe, Omri.

These are the few fragmentary illusions to suicide in the Hebrew Bible. Perhaps because of the extreme rarity of the act, there are no written explicit prohibitions against suicide.

2. MACCABEES

Three references to suicide are found in the Books of Maccabees. Each one relates to martyrdom.

II Maccabees 14:37–41 "There was a certain Razis, one of the elders of Jerusalem . . . Due to his benevolence he was called 'Father of the Jews' . . . Nicanor, wishing to show the animosity he felt toward the Jews, sent more than five hundred soldiers to put him under arrest . . . Preferring to die nobly rather than fall into the hands of a mob of sinners and to be outraged in a manner unworthy of his noble rank, he fell upon his sword."

Nicanor, the commander-in-chief of the Syrian army under King Demetrius I, was sent to Judea in 161 B.C.E. to support the Hellenist party against Judas Maccabeus. Nicanor hated the Jews and placed Razis, a patriotic elder of Jerusalem, un-

der arrest. Lest Razis suffer outrage at the hands of the cap-
tors, "he fell upon his sword."

Another instance of suicide is that of Eleazar the martyr
during the persecutions of the Jews by Antiochus Epiphanes
about 168 B.C.E.

II Maccabees 6:18–31 "Eleazar, one of the foremost
scribes, a man well advanced in years and of most noble
countenance, was compelled to open his mouth in an attempt
to force him to eat swine's flesh. He welcomed death with
glory rather than life with pollution, and of his own free will
went to the rack. Spitting out the food, he became an example of what men should do who are steadfast enough to for-
feit life itself rather than eat what is not right for them to
taste, in spite of a natural urge to live.

"Those who were in charge of the forbidden sacrifice, because they had known the man for such a long time before,
took him aside and urged him privately to bring meat, prepared by himself, which would be proper for him to use, and
to pretend that he was eating the meat of the sacrifice ordered
by the king. Thus he might be saved from death and on account of his old friendship for them he might obtain courte-
ous treatment. He, however, high-minded as always, worthy
of his age, worthy of his superiority of rank, his gray hair so
honorably acquired and his distinguished appearance, because of his fine behavior from childhood and still more
because he followed the holy and God-given laws, declared
himself in no uncertain terms, saying that they should rather
quickly send him forth to Hades.

" 'It is not suitable to my age to pretend, lest many of the
youth think that Eleazar in his ninetieth year has changed to
heathenism. They, because of my pretence and for the sake of
this short span of life, will be led astray through me, and I
shall come to a stained and dishonored old age. Even if for
the present I were to escape the punishment of men, nevertheless I could not escape, either living or dead, the vengeance of the Almighty. Therefore, by departing this life
courageously now, I shall show myself worthy of my old age,
and to young men I shall have left a noble example of how to

die happily and nobly in behalf of our revered and holy laws.'

"After saying this he immediately went to the rack. Then those who but a little time before had held him in good will now changed to hostility, thinking that the words he had just spoken showed that he had taken leave of his senses. As he was dying under the blows, he said with his last sigh, 'The Lord in His sacred knowledge is aware that though I could escape death I now endure terrible suffering in my body under these floggings; yet within my soul I suffer this gladly, because of my reverence for Him.' In this way he died, leaving in his death an example of nobility and a memorial of valor, not only to the young but also to the great majority of his nation."

Another reference is that of a mother and her seven sons.

IV Maccabees 17:1–2 "Certain of the guards declared that when she (mother of seven sons) too was about to be seized and put to death, she flung herself into the fire, so that no one might touch her body. O mother with your seven sons, who broke the violence of the tyrant and rendered his evil decrees futile and demonstrated the nobility of faith!"

Suicide is here invested with nobility when linked with martyrdom. The rabbinic dictum was *Yehareg v'al y'a'bor*— "Let one suffer death rather than transgress."

One of the great martyrs in this period was Eleazar ben Jair, the leader of the Sicarii. Eleazar was a descendant of Judas and the founder of the party of Zealots. With almost a thousand men, women, and children, Eleazar took refuge in the fortress of Masada. When besieged by the Romans, he urged his followers to kill themselves rather than fall into the hands of an unmerciful enemy who would slaughter the combatants, attack the women and sell the children into slavery.

3. JOSEPHUS

Since Josephus' pronouncements on suicide are so significant, his writings will be explored in depth. Flavius Josephus, the great historian, was born in Jerusalem about 37 or 38

C.E. and died in Rome about 100 C.E. In recording the destruction of Eleazar ben Jair's garrison, he expressed admiration for the self-sacrifice displayed and for the contempt of death shown by this great throng of Zealots. However, when his own life was threatened, he took refuge in Jotapata. He was anxious to surrender even when the band of forty soldiers hidden with him preferred to kill one another in a mass suicide. These are Josephus' famous words recorded *in toto* when he tried to dissuade his followers from suicide:

"Upon this, Josephus was afraid of their attacking him, and yet thought he should be a traitor to the commands of God if he died before they were delivered, so he began to philosophize to them in the emergency he was in, and spoke to them as follows. 'O my friends, why are we so earnest to kill ourselves and why do we set our dearest things, the soul and body, at such variance. Does any one say that I am changed? Nay, the Romans are sensible how the matter stands well enough. It is a brave thing to die in war, but only according to the law of war, by the hand of conquerers. If, therefore, I flee from the sword of the Romans, I truly deserve to die by my own sword and my own hand; but if they will spare their enemy, how much more justly ought we to spare ourselves? For it is certainly a foolish thing to do that to ourselves which we quarrel with them for doing to us. I admit that it is noble to die for liberty; but only in war, and at the hands of those who try to take that liberty from us; but now our enemies are neither meeting us in battle, nor killing us. Now, he is equally a coward who wishes not to die when he is obliged to die, and he who wishes to die when he is not obliged to do so. What are we afraid of that we will not go up to the Romans? Is it death? If so, shall we inflict on ourselves for certain what we are afraid of, when we but suspect our enemies will inflict it on us? But some one will say that we fear slavery. Are we then altogether free at present? It may also be said that it is a manly act to kill oneself. No, certainly, but a most unmanly one, as I should esteem that pilot most cowardly, who, out of fear of a storm, should sink his ship of his own accord. Indeed suicide is unknown to the common nature of all animals, and is impiety to God our Creator. For no animal dies by its own contrivance, or by its own means. For the desire of life is a strong law of nature with all; on which account we deem those that openly try to take it away from us to be our enemies, and we take vengeance on those that try to do so by treachery. And do you not think that God is very angry when a man despises what He has bestowed on him? For it is from Him that we have received our being, and we ought to leave it to His disposal to take that being away from us. The bodies of all men are indeed mortal, and created out of corruptible matter; but the soul is ever immortal, and is a part of God that inhabits our bodies. Besides, if any one destroys or misuses the deposit he has received from a mere man, he is esteemed a wicked and perfidious person; and if any one cast out of his own body the deposit of God, can we imagine that He Who is thereby affronted does not know of it? Moreover, our law justly ordains that slaves which run away from their masters shall be punished, though the masters they run away from may have been wicked masters to them. And shall we endeavor to run away from God, Who is the best of all masters, and not think ourselves guilty of impiety? Do not you know that those who depart out of this life according to the law of nature and pay the debt which was received from God, when He that lent it to us is pleased to require it back again, enjoy eternal fame; that their houses and posterity are sure, and that their souls are pure and obedient, and obtain the most holy place in heaven, from whence, in the revolution of ages, they are again sent into pure bodies; while the souls of those whose hands have acted madly against themselves, are received in the darkest place in Hades, and God, Who is their Father, punishes those that offend against either soul or body in their posterity. So God hates suicide, and it is punished by our most wise Legislator. For our laws ordain that the bodies of such as kill themselves shall be exposed till sunset without burial, although it be lawful to bury even our enemies.' "

It is postulated that Josephus was anxious to surrender because he was promised his life by a friend, Nicanor, who was one of the Roman tribunes. The band of forty soldiers had no comrades among the Romans and therefore preferred to kill each other in a mass stroke of suicide. Even though Josephus' motives are suspect, he is quoted again and again and reflected a later traditional Jewish attitude towards suicide. That is: "the bodies of such as kill themselves shall be exposed till sunset without the usual burial rites," "that suicide is an affront to God," and "that the soul received from God is wickedly cast off." Thus we see the influence of Josephus' condemnation of suicide was reflected in the centuries to come.

4. TALMUDIC

Since the practice was rare and unusual, there were casual references to suicide in the Hebrew Bible and the Books of Maccabees. Now that the act had become more frequent, a condemnatory tone is introduced. Where before, "let one suffer death rather than transgress," now in the Talmud (*Shefrit* 84:5) this principle is applied *only* to the sins of idolatry, incest and murder when external pressure to transgress is brought to bear. Only then could martyrdom of self-destruction be preferred.

In Talmudic times, an increasing number of suicides is recorded. The rise is in part due to new general spiritual and social crises as well as the growing Greco-Roman influence. The references to suicide reported in rabbinic literature impart insights into the psychological motives of the act.

The disconcerting story of a gruesome double suicide is reported in connection with a meal. A man who was eager to display his generosity arranged a meal for three of his friends during a famine. He placed three eggs before each of them, but the guests gave the eggs to the child of the host. When the latter discovered that the child was holding the eggs, he struck the youngster so hard that he died. Upon seeing this, the mother of the child committed suicide by jumping from the roof. Her husband soon followed her. Embarrassment and anger led to murder, and murder to suicide.

Several sources report the suicide of children whose parents or masters threatened them with punishment because of some transgression. Since the fear aroused by these threats could have tragic consequences, the rabbis concluded that children should never be threatened with overwhelming punishment. They held that a child be disciplined immediately or not at all.

There are many references to suicide in the religious-legal decisions of the Talmud with accompanying reasons and motivations. Again and again it is repeated that the suicide forfeits his share in the world to come and is denied burial honors. The Talmud decrees that a suicide is to receive no eulogy or public mourning. He is to be buried apart in community cemeteries.

5. MEDIEVAL

In 1565, Joseph Caro, the outstanding Talmudic authority, wrote his compendium of religious practices, the *Shulchan Aruch*. He said: "There is none more wicked than one who has committed suicide. For the sake of one individual was the world created, thus he who destroys one soul is considered as though he had destroyed the whole world. Therefore, one should not attend to him, neither should one rend the garment nor mourn for him who had destroyed himself, nor should a funeral oration be pronounced on his behalf."

Opinion among medieval rabbinic authorities was divided as to whether or not the relatives of a suicide are to observe the prescribed mourning rituals. Maimonides held that these rites belong to the category of ceremonies provided for the honor of the deceased and as such are to be dispensed with in cases of suicide. Nachmanides, however, asserted in his *Torat Ha'adam* that the relatives have a duty to the deceased regardless of the circumstances of death.

An important view of suicide was offered by Rabbi Moses Sofer, one of the leading Halachic authorities in the early nineteenth century. In a responsa, *Chatam Sofer,* he strongly defended the view that relatives should observe mourning rites for an individual who committed suicide. He argued that such an individual cannot be placed in a category with unrepentant sinners. Since the act was perhaps the only sin of which the suicide was guilty, he may not have had time for repentance. Rabbi Moses Sofer further stressed that the rabbi of the community must take the feelings of the relatives into consideration and not expose them to shame. Citing the prevailing custom that the *Kaddish* is not recited for an individual who committed suicide, Rabbi Sofer added that he saw no valid reason for this custom. Another rabbi of the same period argued that the regulations regarding a suicide were intended for cases where the act resulted from heresy, but not when it had been caused by distress.

Many rabbis raised important queries concerning suicide. Some perennial questions: "How do you know that the person really committed suicide, especially if he had not explicitly declared his intent nor performed the act in front of witnesses?" "If an individual was found hanging on a tree, could it not have been an accidental death?" "Are the stringent rules valid for minors or the mentally incompetent?"

The sages realized that there were certain extenuating circumstances where the rigid restrictions and prohibitions could be waived. How can you be certain that it was truly a suicide? Continued Joseph Caro: "Without proof to the contrary, a man is not pronounced to be wicked. If therefore a man was discovered hanged or choked, as far as possible the act of killing should be regarded as the deed of another person and not as his own deed." What about a minor? "If a minor committed suicide, it is considered that he had done the deed unwittingly." It is interesting to note that the matter was even approached from the standpoint of mental illness: "If an adult killed himself and it is evident that the act was prompted by madness, he shall be treated as an ordinary deceased person." Although considered a crime against God, suicide could in some circumstances be explained away and even forgiven.

The question of martyrdom or humiliation is a complex

one. When does one commit suicide as an alternative to persecution? Said Joseph Caro: "If an adult had killed himself
and it is evident that the act was prompted through fear or
terrible desperation as was the case with Saul who feared the
Philistines would act with him as they pleased, he likewise
should be treated as an ordinary deceased person." The Biblical principle of the "Sanctification of God" (*Leviticus*
22:32) was sometimes interpreted to mean that one should
undergo martyrdom rather than be guilty of the denial of
God. Hence, in the time of the Crusades many Jews killed
themselves and their families before the enemy had arrived.
In 1190 in York, England, five hundred Jews committed
suicide to escape persecution. During the Black Death in
1348 when the Jews were held accountable for the epidemic,
many in fear of persecution burned themselves to death. During World War II, Jews actually paid bribes to the guards of
concentration camps for the opportunity of committing suicide and thus escape further torture and harsh treatment.

In martyrdom, however, one was not to hasten his death.
There is the classic story of Hananiah ben Teradyon who
lived during the Hadrianic persecutions. It was the time
when Rome attempted to break the spirit of the Jews by for-
bidding them to study or teach under penalty of death.
Hananiah disregarded this danger and continued to lecture
to his disciples. He was seized by the Romans and sentenced
to burn at the stake. Hananiah protected his mouth from the
flames so as not to hasten his own death by a single moment,
saying: "It is better that He Who has given me my soul
should take it away, rather than I should destroy it myself."

6. MODERN: THE JEWISH ATTITUDE TODAY

The attitude of Reform Judaism is cited by Solomon B.
Freehof, of Pittsburgh, Pennsylvania, in his *Reform Jewish
Practice and Its Rabbinic Background:* "According to Jewish
law one is considered a suicide only when there is absolute
certainty that he premeditated and committed the act with a
clear mind not troubled by some great fear or worry which

might have beset him for the moment and caused him temporarily to lose his mind. In the absence of such certain evidence he is given the benefit of the doubt . . . whenever
possible we should try to spare (the surviving relatives) the
disgrace which would come to them by having their relative
declared a suicide.

"Thus, for example, the great Orthodox authority Moses
Sofer in his # 326 (*Yoreh Dea*) gives many reasons for giving
the alleged suicide the benefit of the doubt as to whether he
should be adjudged guilty of the crime of deliberate self-
destruction; and certainly we should consider the feelings
and reputation of his family.

"In the spirit of the above responsa, it is the general custom among Liberal congregations to bury suicides in their
family plots."

For the Conservative point of view, Rabbi Max Routten-
berg of Rockville Centre, New York wrote: "The Law Committee has generally regarded a suicide as an emotionally distressed and overwrought person, and therefore not responsible for his actions. It would be almost impossible to ascertain
a person's motives and lucidity at the time of such an act. We
are inclined to say that he was not in his right mind at that
time. He is, therefore, given burial and last rites in the same
manner as any other deceased."

For an opinion from an Orthodox Rabbi, there is a communication from Rabbi Samuel Korff of Congregation
Kehillath Jacob in Mattapan, Massachusetts, and the Executive Vice-President of the Vaad Harabonim, the Council of
Orthodox Rabbis: "A general review of Halacha will convince us that a suicidal act cannot be accepted as a 'sane act'
under any circumstances . . . The laws are most liberal in
recognizing the state of mind of the individual and, therefore, the word 'suicide' would never be applied in the following cases: 1. temporary insanity—2. fear—3. pain—4. Sanctification of the Divine Name (during the Crusades, entire Jewish Communities went through a special ritual of divine
blessing in slaughtering one another for they knew that once
captured by the enemy, they would be forced to accept the
Christian faith)."

B. MOHAMMEDANISM

For Mohammedans, suicide is the gravest sin. In committing suicide one violates his *Kismet*. The faithful Moslem awaits his destiny; he does not snatch it from the hands of God. Suicide is expressly forbidden in the *Koran*.

C. JAPANESE RELIGIOUS FAITHS

Suicide reached its greatest proportions in Japan where it was embedded in religious and national tradition. Compulsory suicide was a form of punishment granted only to an offender of noble birth. He could expiate his crime and "save face" by dying at his own hands rather than by the sword of the public executioner. Elaborate ceremonies attended this act. Voluntary *Hara-Kiri* was committed for revenge and for other reasons: to protest the policies of a feudal chief or to follow one's lord into the next world. The entire population has been affected by this practice of the noble Samurai. Many writers feel this tradition is still reflected in Japan's suicide rate—the highest in the world.

D. CHRISTIANITY

Christian views were at first a mixture of Jewish, Hellenistic, and Roman outlooks. Among the Greeks and Romans, suicide was not taboo; indeed, the ancient heroic legends and epic poems often mentioned it with pride. Although some early Greek philosophers did oppose it, those of later schools tended to be more lenient. Suicide was encouraged among the Cynics, Cyrenaics, Stoics and Epicureans. Human life was regarded as relatively unimportant among all these groups— though for various reasons. When Christianity came into being, suicide was very common in Greece and Rome.

The early Christians apparently accepted the prevailing attitudes of their era particularly when persecution made life unbearable. The Apostles did not denounce suicide; the New

Testament touched on the question only indirectly. For several centuries the leaders of the church did not condemn the practice which apparently was rather common.

The earliest disapproval of suicide was expressed by the second Council of Orleans in 533. Churches were permitted to receive the offerings on behalf of those who were killed in the commission of a crime provided they did not lay violent hands on themselves. Suicide was now regarded as the most serious and heinous of all crimes. In 563 the fifteenth Canon of the Council of Braga denied the suicide the funeral rites of the eucharist and the singing of psalms. Augustine, the First Archbishop of Canterbury, who lived about 600 deliberated at great length whether self-destruction could be condoned in the case of a woman whose honor is in danger. Augustine asserted it could not, for "suicide is an act which precluded the possibility of repentance, and it was a form of homicide and thus a violation of the Decalogue Article, 'Thou shalt not kill' and not justified by the above exception." The Council of Hereford in 673 denied burial rites to the suicide and their decision was affirmed by King Edgar in 967. In 1284, the Synod of Nimes refused suicides even the quiet interment in holy ground.

From the Middle Ages until comparatively recently, indignities were often practiced on the corpse of the suicide. The body was dragged through the streets, a stake was driven through the heart and left for carrion birds to destroy. Superstitions grew up about the suicide's corpse and ghost. If a pregnant woman stepped upon the grave of a suicide's corpse, the myth arose that her child would eventually follow the same bitter path. While theological and civil authority were inseparable during this time, the religious-civil prohibition concerning self-destruction was an effective deterrent.

The philosophical currents of the 17th century brought new views of suicide. Religious authority was being questioned and undermined. John Donne, a Protestant apologist for suicide, argued that self-homicide was a sin against the law of self-preservation, but no more. He viewed it as neither a violation of the law nor against reason. Hume, Montaigne,

Montesquieu, Voltaire, and Rousseau wrote essays defending suicide under certain conditions. They argued for the greater freedom of the individual against the authority of the ecclesiastical authorities.

Today, many disciplines have given new insights to the problem of suicide. Even though religion is based upon the concept of the dignity of the individual and the reaffirmation of life, some clergymen view the questions not only from the theological level but the depth psychic causes as well as the sociological implications. Ethical-religious approaches are counter-balanced with the broader perspectives of the social sciences. Increasingly, suicide is being recognized not only as a religious question but a major medical problem.

For this reason, many groups such as the Anglican Church, taking into consideration modern research, have appointed commissions to revise the harsh religious laws with regard to suicide. The Lutheran Church in America does not regard suicide as an "unforgivable sin," and a Lutheran who takes his own life is not denied a Christian burial.

In the Catholic Church, a directive has been issued to the priests in the Archdiocese of Boston relative to Canon 1240 of the *Code of Canon Law* which forbids Christian burial to "persons guilty of deliberate suicide." Richard Cardinal Cushing has interpreted the law in this way: "The Church forbids Christian burial to suicides, but only if they were in full possession of their faculties at the time of the crime. The element of notoriety must be present in a suicide for the penalty to be incurred. Hence, no matter how culpable it may have been, if it is not publicly known that the act was fully deliberate, if the culpability is known only to a few discreet people, burial is not to be denied. Ordinarily there is not too great a difficulty in granting Christian burial to a suicide, since most people these days consider the fact of suicide to be a sign of at least temporary insanity."

Since it is difficult to accurately define "deliberate suicide" and since "most people these days consider the fact of suicide to be a sign of at least temporary insanity," Bishop Thomas J. Riley of St. Peter's Catholic Church in Cambridge has stated that he cannot recall a single case in Massachusetts where Christian burial has been denied a suicide.

E. CONCLUSION

Judaism—and this includes all its branches—is committed to the sanctity of life. One would hope that man not engage in acts of self-destruction. But life is replete with exceptions and contradictions. There are wars and he kills. There are acts of martyrdom and he applauds the heroism of those who refuse to acquiesce to evil even for the sake of living. Religious literature is filled with examples of those who preferred to die for the sanctification of God's name. In addition, modern psychiatry has furnished valuable information as to the person's complex physical and psychological makeup which actually encourage suicidal predispositions.

Who then would further degrade the family of a man who chose death by his own hand? Who would, by an act of not burying the suicide in the cemetery proper, bring added anguish to those already sorely lacerated by unbearable grief?

No one is suggesting that suicide is desirable or commendable. But it must be underscored that we who manipulate nature with nuclear bombs should be less unctuous and more understanding of the actions of our fellowman. Say the sages: "Do not judge your neighbor until you are in his place." For judgments belong to God, not fallible, mortal man. We can only question with the Psalmist: "What is man, O Lord, what is man?"

III. *Psychodynamics of Suicide*

The clergyman should be familiar with the psychiatric literature dealing with suicide. Possessing an understanding of the roots of the problem, he may then be able to detect the symptoms and even prevent self-destruction. Too much misinformation, prejudice, arrogance, fanaticism, and ignorance already exist in this area. Psychological study of attempted suicide would contribute much to the knowledge of psychopathology and serve as a valuable guide in the early recognition and detection of persons with suicidal tendencies.

This section will deal with the concepts of the great psychologists and their opinions on the causes of suicide. From the approaches of Sigmund Freud, Otto Fenichel, Karl Menninger, Carl Jung, Alfred Adler, Harry Stack Sullivan, Karen Horney and others, it is immediately discernible that the suicidal attempt is a complex behavior pattern based on a variety of motivations.

A. THEORETICIANS

1. SIGMUND FREUD

On April 27, 1910, the Vienna Psychoanalytic Society had a discussion on "Suicide in Children." In commenting upon the paper at this meeting, Freud expressed the sentiment that the schools, in their zeal to wean children from their early family life, often erred by exposing the immature student too rapidly and too brusquely to the full severities of adult life. He stated that too little was known about suicide but that perhaps the act was really a renunciation of life because of the craving for death. This remark foreshadowed Freud's later belief in a death instinct.

His paper, *Mourning and Melancholia,* and other future works depicted his psychoanalytic theory of suicide. There are two kinds of drives: one is the life instinct, or *Eros;* the other, the death instinct, or *Thanatos,* the destructive and aggressive drive. The interaction of the Eros and Thanatos constitutes the psychological and biological phenomena of life. The suicidal tendency is the manifestation of the fundamental drive of the death instinct. Sadism is turned against the individual himself: "The ego sees itself deserted by the superego and lets itself die. The Thanatos has far exceeded the Eros and brings self-destruction."

2. OTTO FENICHEL

Other psychiatrists have elaborated upon the Freudian concept of the instinct of aggression. Fenichel extended

Freud's concept. He stated that suicide is the outcome of a strong ambivalent dependence on a sadistic superego and the necessity to rid oneself of an unbearable guilt tension at any price. The superego is that repository of the moral precepts taught by the authority figures—parents, teachers, and clergymen. When this feeling of protection vanishes, the original feeling of annihilation which the person experienced as the deserted, hungry baby reappears.

Since the pressure of the superego is intolerable, there is the tendency toward self-destruction. To live, one must feel a certain self-esteem and support from the protective force of the superego. If the pain is too great, the individual may abandon hope of regaining self-importance. By submission to the punishment of the superego's cruelty, there is the feeling that self-murder will bring about forgiveness and reconciliation. The punishing superego will be destroyed upon regaining a union with the protective superego.

Fenichel mentioned the "partial suicides" where death does not occur directly. One's actions constitute many self-destructive responses of self-punishment. The underlying unconscious mechanism is identical with suicide. Even though death eventually results from the sadistic acts, these "partial suicides" never find their way into the statistics of suicide.

3. KARL MENNINGER

Menninger agrees with Freud that there is the paradoxical contradiction in life of self-preservation and self-destructiveness. He concurs with Fenichel that there are self-destructive impulses which result in "partial suicide." His own close scrutiny of the deeper motives for suicide posits the hypothesis of three elements.

First, there is the impulse derived from the primary aggressiveness crystallized as the *wish to kill*. The mood is reflected in the rage of the baby when his desires are thwarted. There may also be an intense hostility and rivalry toward a loved one: "Just as a suckling child resents weaning and feels that something is taken away from him that it is his right to possess, so these people who are predominantly infantile cannot stand thwarting." The wish to kill is turned back upon the person of the "wisher" and carried into effect as suicide.

Another element is the *wish to be killed*. Just as killing is the extreme form of aggression, so is being killed the extreme form of submission. The demands of conscience are so inexorable that there is no appeasement. In order to expose the ego to punishment, people often put themselves in circumstances in which they must suffer. There is a masochistic desire to atone by being hurt or killed.

A final element is the *wish to die*. These are the impulses of the daredevil drivers or mountain climbers who expose themselves to constant danger. Not only is there the drive for narcissistic gratification but a need for exposure to the ultimate gratification of the death instinct. The consciousness of the wish to die is extremely widespread especially in mental illness. The patient may believe he will find release from mental anguish.

The triumph of the Thanatos over the Eros brings self-destruction. Conversely, if the destructive impulses of the death wish become sufficiently neutralized as to disappear behind the evidences of constructive positive feelings, the result is no longer suicide or homicide, but creation, the *making* of life rather than the *taking* away of life. In this sense, procreation, the act of coitus, is the polar antithesis of murder.

4. CARL JUNG

Jung detects in the suicidal person the unconscious craving for a spiritual rebirth. With the death of the individual, the ego is believed to return to the womb of the mother in order to reestablish contact and there be reborn. Like the psychological factors involved in conversion, there is the desire to escape from that which is perceived by the individual to be intolerable reality. In regression, there is the searching back to that which was considered secure by becoming the infant-newborn.

Carl Jung observed that the symbolic productions of disturbed persons resembled those of primitive peoples. The hereditary portion of the mind contains imprints of ancestral experience—a collective unconscious. The collective unconscious contains the archetype of the crucifixion that is linked with death and its reward of resurrection.

5. ALFRED ADLER

In his psychological theory of suicide, Adler believed that the individual was directed by one over-all striving. The goal is success, defined in the person's own subjective terms. Certain characteristics are akin to both suicide and mental disorders. Like depression, suicidal tendencies develop "in individuals whose method of living from early childhood has been dependent upon the achievements and the support of others. They will always try to lean on others." They are pampered, spoiled—poor losers. They expect everyone to understand them, while they care nothing about understanding others. They desire love as a matter of course but seldom give love in return. They would say: "I love you because I need you"; never, "I need you because I love you."

The suicidal patient has feelings of inferiority and little confidence. Because of this lack of self-esteem, he is ego-centered rather than problem- or other-centered. Suicide is his veiled attack upon others. By an act of self-destruction, he hopes to evoke sympathy and compassion and bring reproach to those who he feels have hurt him.

6. HARRY STACK SULLIVAN

Sullivan postulates an inter-personal theory of psychology. Even as electrons are moved by magnetic attractions, so individuals are motivated responsively to other persons who are significant to them. The crucial point is the individual's relationship to other people. The growing infant has three personifications of "me." In his security, he is the "good me"; in anxiety, he is the "bad me"; in the psychotic nightmares, he is the "not me." The child evaluates himself in terms of the significant others' reactions toward him.

When the security of the self is threatened, the acute anxiety is labeled *dissociation* (as opposed to the Freudians who use the word *repression*.) Because of dissociation, because of the anxieties of life, because of the unresolved conflicts, because of the "bad me," and especially the "not me," mental disorders occur often manifested by suicidal attempts. Such predispositions for suicide are caused by a depressive syndrome of the self-deprecating patient. Suicide reflects a hostile integration in society with other persons. Self-destruction is a derogatory and hostile attitude directed against other people—the outer world—and is finally directed with full force against the self.

7. KAREN HORNEY

Although first trained as a Freudian analyst in Germany, Horney later broke with the classical psychoanalytic movement and rejected Freud's instinct theory. Were the infant given an anxiety-free environment, she said, he would grow and prosper. However, culture, religion, politics, and other similar forces conspire to produce distorted forms of the child's self-development.

The insecure child thinks of the world as a hostile place in which to live. This causes a *basic anxiety*. To cope with this, he may assume any one or a combination of approaches for a solution to his disturbed needs. In the zeal to overcome basic anxieties, he develops feelings of power, of supremacy, of exploitation of others, of personal admiration, of self-sufficiency, of perfection, and unassailability.

There are other contradictory demands which he hopes will also overcome his anxieties—the need for affection and a partner who will share his life. A vicious circle develops. In the thrust for power and independence, he alienates the people who might give him the desired love and admiration. The idealized self-image, the godlike being, hates the actual self, the real self, yet has to depend upon it for support and maintenance. In a patient's own words: "The only difficulty I have is reality."

The inner conflict involves the battle between the constructive forces of the real self and the obstructive forces of the idealized self. The idealized self punishes the actual self because of renewed evidences and reminders of inadequacy. The result is hatred of the divided self, with eventual destruction and self-imposed death.

Heroism and bravery give the idealized self a reinforced sense of importance. If the action fails and there is no glory, self-destruction comes as a punishment for the failure. An example of this could be death in battle. A slower form of suicide occurs when the idealized self invests the real self with ugliness and slothfulness, degrading that actual self and allowing it to die. This is readily detected in the alcoholic person whose self-degradation is part of the punishment which he feels is his due. In the desire for punishment, the alcoholic provokes others into rejecting him. A core of abject self-hatred is combined with an outer armor of arrogant defiance. Karen Horney's idea of therapy would involve help in realistically facing the real self by replacing the idealized self with healthy growth.

B. PSYCHOLOGICAL RESEARCH

1. CLUES TO POTENTIAL SUICIDE

As clergymen without thorough knowledge and tools of depth psychology, it is essential to understand some of those situations where suicide may be contemplated and attempted. The rabbi may not be familiar with the battery of tests such as the Thematic Apperception Test (T.A.T.), the Sentence-Completion Test, the Minnesota Multiphasic Personality Inventory (M.M.P.) which have had some degree of success in the suicide prevention centers. However, he should be aware of some of the possible admonitions and clues. According to studies, the potential suicide gives definite warnings. With alertness and knowledge, the clergyman can meet the challenge of the 10th killer—the cruelest death of all in terms of those who remain.

There are diverse aspects of the pre-suicidal phase. Each symptom alone does not designate a potential suicide. Combined over a considerable period, the prodromes are a danger signal to which the wise therapist is alerted:

*Insomnia caused by deep depression.

*Loss of appetite and interest in food, loss of weight; (all foods taste alike—like sawdust); low calorie intake; constipation.

*Loss of interest and "drive"; loss of interest in family, hobbies, recreation; sexual impotence, frigidity.

*Moodiness, refusal to admit despondency. Tactful questions bring the answer, "I feel bad all over."

*Excessive use of barbiturates. Addiction follows efforts to overcome insomnia.

*Open threats to suicide. (They never should be ignored.)

*Absence of affection and the presence of a deep-seated hostility to those normally close to the subject.

Philip Solomon, Associate Clinical Professor of Psychiatry at Harvard Medical School, has devised a method of quantifying the risk involved in suicide by grouping them according to their seriousness.

"Any *one* of these signs indicates serious risk:

*Severe depression—The most common precursor of suicide.

*Psychosis—Withdrawal, confusion, depersonalization.

*Desire for death—'I wish I were dead.'

Any *two* of these signs indicate serious risk:

*Previous suicide attempt—May be made a second time.

*Violent method chosen—Threat of buying a gun or a knife to slash his throat.

*Suicide letter.

*Isolation from people.

*Previous psychosis.

Any *three* of these signs indicate serious risk:

*Bankruptcy.

*Chronic maladjustment—Poor personal relationships, delinquency, or criminality.

*Alcoholism.

*Over 40 years of age.

*Male."

2. CAUSATIVE FACTORS IN SUICIDE

When an epidemiologist sets out to determine the causes of a disease, he does not conceive of a single root—some virus, bacillus or germ. Rather he conceives of a constellation of factors or circumstances in a special set of interrelationships involved in producing a disease process. Host factors relate to the nature of the organism that undergoes the disease process. Then there are environmental factors—the conditions surrounding the host—which encourage or inhibit the agent.

The epidemiological model of disease can be useful in a study of the factors of suicide by imparting direction to variables and interactions. Suicidal behaviors occur in many circumstances in different types of people and for many apparent motives.

a. *Host Factors*

The host factors for suicidal behavior include those characteristics in the person himself: everything about his psychological makeup which encourages suicidal predispositions, impulses, or plans.

What type of person could believe that self-destruction is a solution—formidable as it may be, but a solution nonetheless —to life's problems?

(1) Loneliness

The personality factor is essential to an understanding of suicide. Everyone faces the problem of living in a socially disorganized and disrupted world. Not all, however, seek flight from reality through self-killing. Very often the person most prone to suicide possesses a sensitive and solitary personality. He feels insecure and unloved. In cases of attempted suicide cited by Palmer, friendships were not easily made. Loneliness and spite feelings were marked. One-fifth of the suicides in London, according to another study by Hopkins, fit into the "forlorn" category. Among the attempted suicides in Scotland, a feeling of loneliness, of being a burden to others, or of feeling unwanted are found in 23 out of 40 cases. A broken home in childhood also plays a significant role in suicidal attempts. Because of a feeling of rejection, a lack of love and supervision, the person just does not seem to care about living.

(2) Defective and Punitive Superego

Experiences in early childhood often damage the superego and lead the way to suicidal tendencies. Norman Tabachnik in his article, *Observation on Attempted Suicides,* discusses the correlation of parental severity and superego strength. He cites the recurring pattern of disturbance and difficulty in early childhood with a dominant and overpowering mother or mother surrogate which results in suicidal tendencies. The mother gives affection to the child when the offspring is "good." The price for her attention is obedience, with the penalty of anger or dissatisfaction if the child is "bad." The mother's love is conditioned. The offspring's superego is associated with parental severity. In punishment, the child constantly berates himself for the loss of his mother's affection.

In other cases, the mother is seen as an aloof person, removed from the child, concerned with her own selfishness and emotional difficulties. Her withholding of love or incapacity for love causes a weak and defective superego formation. On one hand the withholding of love by the mother results in a *defective* superego; on the other hand, there is the consequence of a *punitive* superego because of the mother exacting affection at a high price.

(3) Fear of Death

An interesting concept of suicide is that of a counterphobic reaction in Thanatobia, the fear of death. The anticipation of death is so horrible that the individual prefers to end these perseverating maudlin concepts by "getting it over with," rather than running away from it. This may be compared to the boy who tries to kill himself to determine if death is as bad as he had thought.

(4) Self-Deprecation and the Need for Escape to New Life

To some, death connotes survival and new beginnings. It is like running away from home. It is rebirth. The "bad me" is eliminated and a new start is made. The hope is for a surcease from the pain of the universe so the deceased, like Romeo and Juliet, may be joined with his loved one in a better life. Or in death, he believes he acquires new powers not possessed by the living, as a ghost or spirit wreaking vengeance upon his enemies. Schilder, Massermann and Zilboorg regarded suicide as a manifestation of life-preserving tendencies.

Death may be conceived of as being a doorway to a new life, or as rest and peaceful sleep. Lord Balfour said before his demise: "This is going to be a great experience." In Homer's *Iliad*, Sleep, *Hypnos*, and Death, *Thanatos*, are alluded to as "twin brothers." (Have religionists perhaps over-romanticized and glorified the meaning of death?)

Despair and loss of self-esteem often accompany the loss of a loved one. The survivor identifies himself with the departed. Zilboorg has suggested that the death of a parent occurring early in a child's life determines the suicidal tendencies later in life. A child's reaction to death or removal is especially severe and intense in the pre-Oedipal period. The longing to be reunited with a dead loved one becomes so overwhelming that the person hopefully contemplates how this reunion might take place. Great is the desire for togetherness in death.

(5) Strong Sense of Guilt and Aggression

The wish for death may contain not only a striving for a fantasied immortality or an urge to test death to ascertain its quality. It could well be the unconscious need to reduce personal guilt through a painful experience (as the woman who is praised for her courage in being married to an alcoholic ne'er-do-well because for her, suffering satisfies a need for punishment for her guilt feelings).

Suicide is a type of vicarious atonement with the acting out of the motor impulses upon the self. Because of the excessive severity of the ego, the aggression is first turned inward in somatic complaints and then in suicidal tendencies which avoid or bring further punishment.

Suicide is geared to relieve one's own guilt and induce guilt upon others. In the act of suicide, the wish is to punish the so-called guilty people, or the introjected parents whom one may wish to murder, or the society itself which is felt to be responsible. The person may muse like a child: "They'll be sorry when I am gone!" Since murder is taboo, for with it is the fear of punishment, the aggression is turned to the self. In Freud's words: "No one can find the psychical energy to kill oneself in the first place unless he is therefore killing at the same time someone with whom he has identified himself, and is directing against himself a death wish which had previously been directed against the other person."

(6) Depression and Mental Illness

The majority of potential suicides suffer from depression. However, there are many cases when depression is not present. An over-simplication is to state that depression is the sole cause and symptom. In one study, only 70 per cent of cases of suicide occurred with patients who were depressed.

Others evidenced such clues as delusions, hallucinations, and irritability which occur in the clinical groups of depressive states and organic dementias. The suicidal rate among schizophrenics is disproportionately high as is the ratio in the manic-depressive grouping. This is not to say that one who has a mental illness will take his life. Each case is different as is the cause for the patient's inability to endure stress and tension. More important than the malady itself is the behavior of the individual. Non-suicidals are generally more passive and receptive to hospital environment.

b. *Environmental Factors*

Environmental factors relate to the pressures of the current life situation which further the development and acting out of suicidal ideas. External situations which precipitate a desire for death include disappointment in love—a fertile cause of adolescent suicide; a consequence of an illicit sex relationship; sickness; the separation from a loved one. Because of outward circumstances, the person feels that he has reached the limit of his resources. He seeks an escape from an intolerable life situation.

c. *Means of Suicide*

The method used in self-destruction often indicates some of the underlying reasons precipitating the suicide. Drowning may reveal the unconscious infantile fantasy regarding "water." The ocean is poetically referred to as mother love. He feels the need to be rocked in his mother's lap and return to her as a child "bathed in goodness." Or drowning might represent the "plunging in" like the smoothness and sudden shock of entering a woman's body. In this context, to go into water is to go into a woman.

Suicide by self-crucifixion is the obvious identification with Jesus. The person also tries to share in the messianic kingdom of immortality.

The taking of poison represents the great intensification of the erotic function of the mouth. This organ is connected with a pathological exaggeration of the need for love received in the infantile way.

These then are some of the dynamics involved in the suicidal person. Since personality is not static and is constantly modified and adjusted to the inner and outer demands of the individual, so the psychological analysis of suicide cannot be reduced to an oversimplified formula but may be understood only in a total picture of life.

IV. *Sociological Approaches to Understanding Suicide*

Spinoza said: *Omne determinato est negatio*—"any definition is a limitation." Psychology has afforded new insights concerning traits, feelings, and actions of mind and personality. Necessary also is comprehension of the forms, institutions, and functions of the man and his associations. While different from any other, each man shares some similarity in communication to the concentric order of the special group.

Sociologists affirm that there is significance in the social milieu in which the infant is born. Customs and institutions have meaning and purpose in meeting the distinctive needs of its members. Both personality and culture derive from the interplay between human needs and the external world. To be sure, there is the individual and his instinctual drives, but these must be understood in light of the unique physical, economic, and political conditions of the group's life force. As Veblen, Pareto, and Thurman Arnold demonstrated, the person's thinking is clothed both by his biological equipment and his adjustment to his world as understood through his family and social hierarchies. Life is more than a haphazard assortment of artifacts joined together in a fortuitous manner.

No man is an island unto himself. In a sense, self-destruction reflects the relationship of the person not only to himself but to his community and society. Suicide becomes more understandable when viewed in conjunction with social facts such as marital status, economic position, race, and religion. Of particular significance is the group attitude to civilization. Is suicide tolerated or prescribed? Much is contingent upon the competitiveness of the culture in which the individual lives and the culture's attitude, for example, towards martyrdom. The captain who goes down with his ship is a reflection of socially and culturally imposed mores.

Just as it is practically impossible to distinguish a potential suicide by the details of case history alone, so is the present sociological data by itself inconclusive. Valid controls are lacking. Cause-and-effect relationships are virtually impossible to isolate. There are no ready-made panaceas to one single question. We do know, however, that society does help direct the sentiments and activities of individuals.

The most important sociological contribution to the understanding of the subject appeared in the work, *Le Suicide,* by Emile Durkheim published in 1897. Durkheim asserted that suicide, which was then generally considered a highly individual phenomenon, was explicable through the social setting. Society, he said, is an entity greater than the sum of its parts, i.e., the individuals and their material fragments. He believed that a group acquires a collective conscience. The degree of suicide is a derivative of that society. The breakdown of collective conscience indicates a basic flaw within the social fabric.

Essentially, Emile Durkheim argued that suicide occurs when an individual feels that he has lost his function in society and can no longer identify with the collective representation. When he has little sense of "belonging" and the relational systems which tie him to people have broken sufficiently, he may wish to be free of living. Life may be experienced then as mainly a task and a burden. Suicide is dependent upon the degree to which the person lacks involvement. He was successful in tying suicide—the act of one individual—to a set of social circumstances through a set of brilliant fundamental constructs.

It was Durkheim's belief that there are three theoretical types of suicide. In *egoistic* suicide, morbid individualism evolves because of a relaxation of religious, family, political, and social controls. Self-destruction occurs when the individual is not sufficiently integrated into his society. There is also the *anomic* (*anomie,* meaning "lawlessness") suicide which represents the failure of the person to adjust to social change. This characteristic is found in times of business crises such as an economic depression or even in an era of prosperity when the *nouveau riche* is unable to adjust to new standards of living. Lastly is the *altruistic* suicide where the group's authority over the individual is so compelling that the individual loses his own personal identity and wishes to sacrifice his life for his group. An example is the soldier who gives his life happily and willingly for his country.

Parenthetically, Henry and Short have recently reviewed demographic data to test the Durkheimian hypothesis. The theories still hold up very well. For example, suicide rates are higher in urban than in rural areas. Holding the effects of age and sex constant, the suicide rate for married persons is also much lower than that for single, widowed, or divorced ones.

A. SUICIDE AND ECONOMIC CONDITIONS

Suicide rates are relatively high among the highest income groups. In the figures for suicide by social class during the period of prosperity of 1920–1923 and of the depression of 1930–1932, the greatest increase occurred among the more prosperous classes. Two-thirds of the variation of the suicide rate in the United States is attributed to severe economic loss. Those with higher status positions react more violently to fluctuations of business than do persons in subordinate status categories. Since poverty is already an accepted fact for them, the indigenous poor are able to adjust to economic depressions with greater equanimity.

Another reason for a higher suicide rate among the privileged groups in American society is that leadership brings greater tensions and frustrations of responsibilities. Self-destruction offers itself as a means of escaping painful anxieties. Commissioned officers in the United States Army kill themselves with greater frequency than the enlisted men of the same race.

B. SUICIDE AND WAR

It must not be assumed that all adversities breed self-destruction. A study of pre-war, war, and post-war suicide rates in ten countries indicates that in every case, suicide was less frequent from 1915 to 1918 and more frequent again from 1926 to 1930. The major emphasis during wartime is that each one—male and female, white and black, old and young—is needed for the great effort of victory.

In war, the youth are able to give vent to their aggressive drive. They are rewarded for destruction through citation of medals and accolades. They are able to achieve the primitive craving for power with the uniforms they wear. In Freud's own words: "The willingness to fight may depend upon a variety of motives which may be lofty, frankly outspoken, or unmentionable. The pleasure in aggression and destruction is certainly one of these. The death instinct would destroy the individual were it not turned upon objects rather than the self, so that the individual saves his own life by destroying something external to it."

C. SUICIDE AND MARITAL STATUS

When the factor of age is held constant, the suicide rate up to the age of 35 is higher for the widowed than for the single person. From the age of 35, the rate of suicide of the single person is higher than that of the widowed. Divorced men and women have a higher suicide rate than the undivorced of the same sex. When one is single, widowed, divorced, or separated, there is often the feeling of aloneness, depression, guilt, hostility, and in some instances loss of patterns of conduct. Suicide is contemplated as an alternative to the difficulties of life.

D. SUICIDE—MALE AND FEMALE

Successful suicides are higher among men than women, but attempted suicides are higher among women. For committed suicides the percentages of male and female are 70 and 30, respectively; whereas for attempted suicides the percentages for males and females are 31 and 69—an almost exact reversal. The answer frequently given for these facts is that men, because of their involvement in business and professional life, are more affected by competition of the external world. The woman's feeling of worthwhileness is more dependent upon the inner world, i.e., children, house, cooking.

Men usually commit suicide by shooting or hanging. Women almost always use passive means of self-destruction: sleeping pills, poisons or gas. They prefer not to shed their blood or disfigure their bodies or cannot abide the thought of making an "awful mess" in their tidy homes.

E. SUICIDE AND AGE

Suicide rates rise sharply with age, from a low point of 4.5 in the 15–24 year group to 27.0 in the 65 and over group, staying at this level to age 85 and over. Children to age 15 practically never take their lives, while from 15 on there is a consistent rise in suicides. Two-thirds of the male suicides and more than half of the female suicides are over 45 years of age.

Statistical tables demonstrate a rise in the frequency of cases of mental depression about the age of the 40's when significant changes are taking place. With menopause and climacteric, come the psychological reverberations creating rigidity and intolerance. Goals of life have been attained or just seem unattainable. In Carl Jung's words: "The neurotic is a person who can never have things as he would like them in the present and who could never enjoy the past." There is a short step from frustration to cynicism and vice versa. Early anxieties are aggravated by failures in middle life with intimate marital and familial conflicts. As persons reach middle age and friends of contemporary ages pass on, there is often the dread of death as well as concern for the health and welfare of loved ones. The elderly are prone to arteriosclerotic and senile states with the involutional form of mental disorder. Suicide is attributed to physical pain, mental illness, loneliness, and lack of meaning in life. Since death may not be far off, and since the degenerative diseases are reaching the mortal climax, self-destruction is contemplated as a solution to the inevitable.

F. SUICIDE AND YOUTH

Suicide ranks fourth as the cause of death among the general adolescent population. From age 15 to 19, the male suicide rate is 5.5 per 100,000 and 2 per 100,000 for girls. Among college students, suicide has become the second most frequent root of death surpassed only by accidents.

"Pressures starting from early childhood are the one important motivation of suicide," states the American Orthopsychiatric Association. Attempts of young people to end their lives are based on depressed feelings of being rejected, abandoned, and unable to meet competition.

Dr. Rita V. Franiel, Acting Director of the Columbia College Counseling Service, believes that the present college generation is a lonely one and loneliness brings suicide. Many of today's college students are the war babies of the 1940's and are likely to come from homes broken by divorce and separation. She asserted: "Alienated lonely people breed alienated lonely people; the parents cannot get close to their children and they breed in their children a fear of getting close to people. Suicidal college students have options of people to talk to about their problems, but the difficulty is making them trust people to whom they can talk."

An anxiety of youth is being able to compete successfully in school. Failure to achieve brings dissatisfaction and disappointment from parents as well as low ego-strength of oneself.

Pressure, loneliness, depression, lack of trust and faith, inability to communicate—these are the hallmarks of suicidal young people.

G. SUICIDE AND NEIGHBORHOOD

The suicide rate in the United States falls steadily from its high point in cities of over 100,000 population to its low point in rural areas. This is attributed to the psychic aggravations and complications of city life. The model suicide committer and attempter in Los Angeles County for 1957 lived in an apartment or an apartment-house area. In the constant mobility, the individual lacks social organization, roots, and a sense of belonging.

Pacific Coast cities like Seattle, Portland, Oakland, Los Angeles, and San Francisco have exceedingly high suicide rates. The highest is San Francisco with a rate 2½ times that of the nation as a whole. Two Florida cities, Miami and St. Petersburg, with a large number of elderly and invalided people also have high suicide rates, about twice the national average estimated at 13.5 per 100,000. There are more suicides of persons living in high-rent areas in Chicago than in low-rent areas. Many southern cities such as Chattanooga and Knoxville, Tennessee; Corpus Christi, Texas; and Greensboro, North Carolina boast low suicide rates, mainly because they are peopled by a goodly proportion of Negroes, who rarely take their own lives.

H. SUICIDE AND THE NEGRO

Whites are three times more likely to kill themselves as Negroes. However, as Negroes migrate to Northern industrial centers, the rate of suicides among Negro men rises markedly. The difficulty he experiences in integrating himself into a differing society—a step for which he is not sufficiently prepared—leads to *egoistic* self-destruction. He also becomes more prone to *anomic* suicide due to the higher self-expectations and problems in economic adjustment attendant upon a closer relationship with the Caucasian community.

I. SUICIDE AND OCCUPATION

The kind of job held is clearly a factor in suicides. University of Oregon researchers studied self-inflicted deaths in Oregon between 1950 and 1961. They found suicides among doctors, dentists, and lawyers three times as common as among non-professional white-collar workers.

Professional men, such as physicians, army officers, actors, and political figures commit suicide in greater proportion than do those who look up to them for guidance and strength. Anxieties are caused by oppressive responsibility and the leading of complicated and frenetic lives. Academic knowledge does not presuppose cohesiveness in family life or an integration of personality.

J. SUICIDE AND MONTH

More suicides occur in the spring when one's bleak feelings are confronted by the bloom and burgeoning of nature. The contrast of one's unhappiness with the bleakness of winter is not nearly so sharp as the contrast of the bright days and the dark self. Historically, spring neuroses are identified with the old seed-sowing festivals and the explosive accompaniment of wine, women, and song. The sharp dichotomy between the smiling spring world and the despairing state of mind is one of the factors in determining the act of one's self-destruction. As the poet T. S. Eliot once said, "April is the cruelest month of all." The April suicide rate is the highest for any month and is some 120 per cent above the average for the rest of the year.

K. SUICIDE AND COUNTRY

A striking feature of suicide statistics is the wide difference in rates between countries. Denmark, Sweden, Japan, and Hungary have more than twice the United States rate; while Ireland, Costa Rica, and some other nations have one-fourth or one-fifth the United States rate. The differences are hard to explain. Some observers, including former President Eisenhower, have suggested that cradle-to-grave social security systems may cause unhappiness and contribute to suicide in Denmark and Sweden. But Norway, also a highly socialized land, has a lower rate than the United States, and the high rates in Denmark go back a century or more, predating the welfare state.

L. SUICIDE AND RELIGIOUS AFFILIATION

Emile Durkheim said that religious affiliation is a strong influence in determining habits of thought as well as one's philosophy of life. Religions attempt to answer in divergent ways the perplexing enigmas: "Is life a gift of God?" "Does man have the moral right to take his own life?" "Are we accountable to a Supreme Deity?" "What is the meaning of our suffering?" "Does life have purpose?" "Is there a belief in a world beyond?" "Does suicide hasten or deny entry into a future world?" "Can suicide be heroic, justifiable?" "Is self-destruction unconscionable?"

Suicides have been a part of traditional religious rites in Japan, China, India, and many widely scattered religious tribes. As indicated, in Japan the method of *Hara-Kiri* had been widely publicized during World War II when Japanese soldiers would take their own lives to avoid the disgrace of capture by the enemy. Rather than a demise of shame, the body was buried with solemn respect near the Buddhist temples. Suicides known as *Junshi* also occurred. As an act of loyalty, a servant would take his own life upon the death of his lord so as to follow the master into the next world.

Many studies have been formulated to determine the relationship of suicide to religious affiliation. The *Jewish Encyclopedia* states that in most countries, the frequency of suicides according to religion occur in this order: Protestants, Catholics, and Jews. Durkheim believed that the suicide rate for Catholics and Jews was approximately the same. However, since the variables cannot be isolated, no definitive proofs are verifiable.

For example, in comparison rates for the early 1950's in Europe certain Catholic countries had low rates (the rates are the number of suicides per 100,000 population): Spain, 5.4 and the Republic of Ireland, 2.7; in contrast Catholic Belgium had a rate of 13.6; France, 15.1. Protestant countries similarly fluctuated with Norway, 7.5 to Denmark, 23.3. Obviously factors other than religion are important, i.e., economics, educational level, rural or urban countries, and peace or war.

Variables are found in Austria where the Jews at one time were economically poor and socially isolated. The number of suicides per one million Jews was but 20.7; on the other hand in Baden and Bavaria where the Jew was on a higher plane economically and socially, the rate was a high as 140, about seven times more frequent than in Austria. The Jew reflected the mores of the country as witnessed by the higher suicide rate among the Christians in Baden and Bavaria.

It is important to note that in Israel in 1949, about the time of the war with the Arab countries, the suicide rate was 7.1, out of 100,000 population. Dr. Dublin reports suicide rates in Israel are still relatively low, not only among newcomers (among them, those liberated from the camps) but in the entire Jewish population (8 per 100,000 in 1952 to 10 per 100,000 in 1958). Males have a higher rate than females. A high proportion of suicides suffer from mental illness, especially schizophrenia.

Before the State of Israel, with the coming of Hitler, his program of extermination, and the demoralizing influences of another World War, suicide among Jews grew to epidemic proportions. Suicide epidemics among Jews were recorded in Poland, Germany, and Austria beginning in the 1920's. They increased to "fantastic levels" in Germany and among the populations awaiting deportation. Suicide was wide-spread among the Jews of Holland and Norway after the Nazi invasion.

In the concentration camps, suicide rates were lower by comparison. Dr. Dublin takes a practical view of the reasons: "Those who retained some strength cherished hopes of ultimately joining their families; as they weakened, they had neither the necessary mental or physical strength, nor the means to do away with themselves." There was an increase in suicide "among those who were liberated at the end of the war when they realized the full horror of their recent experience."

Religious factors could in some degree influence the frequency of suicide. Durkheim's hypothesis of the comparative immunity of Catholics to suicide was attributed to the individual's integration into the church through a body of common sentiments and beliefs. The church helped to give an historical ready-made solution to many perplexing personal problems. According to some authorities, this would explain the high suicide rate among the multifactioned and loosely-federated Protestants.

In Judaism, there are sociological as well as religious reasons which could account for a lower suicidal rate. The family has been the strong foundation of the Jewish social structure. In Mark Twain's words, "The Jewish home is a home in the truest sense." The family is the germinal cell whence come spiritual and ethical values. Trust and faith are expressed not only by the language of words but the language of human relationships. Sociologists often attribute the small percentage of criminality, alcoholism, and sexual promiscuity to the solidarity of the Jewish family.

In a monograph by the Yale Center of Alcohol Studies written by Charles R. Snyder, entitled *Alcohol and the Jews:* "All the evidence from both European and American sources indicates that in the Jewish group, drinking pathologies are rare." Among non-Jews, suicide is often directly and indirectly traceable to the abuse of alcoholic beverages. Suicide due to drunkenness is very rare among the Jews. Even the fact that the Jews were persecuted through the centuries did not increase the ratio of their suicides. William James once said: "Sufferings and hardships do not as a rule abate the love of life; they seem on the contrary, usually to give it a keener zest." Prosperity often brings suicide in its train, and the Jews were seldom afforded the luxury of security. Jewish history is replete with suffering, stake, torture, inquisition, auto-da-fé. Life was more than the slings and arrows of outrageous fortune. The Jew considered himself the mirrored image of God commanded to imitate Him—to perform His *Mitzvot,* to hallow His name and to advance His kingdom. Life was to be lived even with adversity. God's world was still unutterably beautiful. "The heavens declare the work of God and the firmament proclaims His handiwork."

Judaism is life-centered. Eschatology is weakly developed

in Jewish theology while ethics is strongly accentuated. The Jewish heritage is an action-oriented religion. The way one lives today determines one's future salvation, yet there is no excessive preoccupation with rewards in the after-life. The toast over wine is *l'Chayim*—"To Life." The first letter of the word signifying life—*Chai*—is worn as a kind of amulet. The life-centered Jew who in times of personal crisis contemplates suicide is traditionally reminded to recall the much greater hardships suffered by his co-religionists. To value his own life so little as to destroy it is in a sense to identify with those who devalued the lives of his martyred ancestors.

In Judaism, the emphasis is on the tasks and duties of *this* life. A variety of intimations of immortality have been taught through the centuries but without dogmatic creed. Joseph Albo in his *Book of Roots* (1413) drew attention to the relative importance of the Christian concept of resurrection in contrast to Judaism. In Christianity, the crucifixion is considered a cornerstone of the entire edifice of its faith. In the words of Paul, "But if there is no resurrection of the dead, then Christ has not been raised; if Christ has not been raised, then our preaching is in vain and your faith is in vain." (I *Cor.* 15:13 ff)

The act of suicide is often considered a desire for resurrection and rebirth. According to Henderson's *Text Book of Psychiatry*, potential suicides often believe that God has commanded them to destroy themselves even as Jesus was crucified. Jung mentioned the potential suicidal need for spiritual rebirth.

Pastoral Psychology devoted its entire December, 1953 issue to "Christmas and Suicide," a discussion of birth and rebirth. L. Bryce Boyer analyzed how some of his patients identified themselves with the baby Jesus at this time of year, and his eventual death that the faithful might live. Christmas was part of a "holiday" syndrome distinguished by a desire for a new birth like Jesus and a magical resolution of the unsettled problems of life.

Despite these hypotheses, it is impossible to determine exactly the relationship between suicide and religious affiliation. Today, the ghetto walls have crumpled and those religious and ethnic differences that separated peoples are gradually disappearing. Religious statistics are difficult to compile. In California, the death certificate does not indicate one's religion. The compilation of data is woefully incomplete. Even the word, *Jew,* or *Protestant,* or *Catholic* is deceiving and deceptive. Is he a practicing Jew? Does the Catholic attend Mass? Is the word, *Protestant,* a mark of commitment or a facile title implying "Miscellany"?

The point is self-manifest: on the basis of the statistical study of the relationship between suicide and religious affiliation, simple deductions cannot be effectively tabulated as a single dimensional technique. Just as there are differences between religions regarding the judgment of suicide, so there are differences of attitudes and sociological changes even within the same religion over a period of time. Clearly, the suicide rate is influenced by many factors besides the religion of its population—economic conditions, social traditions, degree of urbanization, and even the prevailing political climate.

V. *Counseling the Potential Suicide*

Suicide is a desperate affair. It is ugly for onlookers, devastating for relatives, and harrowing for those professionally concerned. One's ideas about suicide usually have an emotional tinge, but when confronted with it, an even stronger dimension is added—overwhelming fear.

Somebody who chooses self-destruction brings death dramatically in front of his fellowmen and forces it into their thoughts. So repugnant is the idea that the subject of suicide is studiously avoided or discussed in frightened, horrified whispers.

Unfortunately, some doctors do not show equal concern for the suicidal person as they do for surgical and medical patients. They feel that self-killing is the individual's own business and each person is entitled to die as he wishes. So, also, is the rabbi's relationship to the potential suicide uncontrollably affected by his general attitude toward suicide. Many religious leaders regard suicide with feelings of prejudice, arrogance, and a fanaticism based on misinformation. The reaction may include indifference and apathy: "It's very clear to me; you're just making those threats to gain attention." Or the other end of the spectrum where he demonstrably exhorts and sermonizes: "You can't do that! It's against God and the faith!"

But suicide is not the only means by which human beings seek to destroy themselves; many turn to submeditated suicide as a means of shortening their lives. It is essential that the religious leader be aware of the signs and prepared to cope with the problem, for submeditated suicide may be less obvious, but it is just as prevalent; less direct, but just as deadly.

The attitudes of the religious leader often will be communicated to the highly sensitive, troubled person. Unless deep-seated prejudgments are uprooted by knowledge and experience, making a genuine acceptance of the disturbed possible, the clergyman will not be able to minister properly and effectively.

The potential suicide is still a child of God. Just as His love is unconditional, so should His children's be, as well as His representatives' who speak in His name. No one who has witnessed the shock and grief occasioned by the loss of a loved one though self-killing can view the possibility and threat of suicide with indifference.

As a result of studies, Schneidman and Farberow have related that it is not always possible to distinguish a potential suicidal person. However, there are guideposts that the pastor may recognize: deep depression, excessive weeping, frequent use of barbiturates, loss of interest, of appetite and of weight, insomnia, restless pacing, wringing of the hands. Eli Robins and his associates in St. Louis have underscored the thought that the suicidal act generally does not come suddenly and without warning. Rather the individual has already given many clues and indications.

The *Medical Tribune* states: "Studies in San Francisco, Philadelphia, and other cities indicate that more than 70 per cent of the persons who commit or attempt suicide are or recently have been under a physician's care. Moreover, careful investigation has revealed that in a large percentage of cases, these suicidal tendencies were expressed verbally or in behavior by the patient before the act."

The religious leader is not a physician, but this does not preclude a responsibility to be more knowledgeable in the area of suicidal symptoms. Alertness to these warnings could well save lives. In Jewish literature it is said: "He who saves one life, it is imputed to him by God, as if he saves the world."

The best clue to the potential suicide is the actual threat itself. Louis Linn and Leo W. Schwarz tell of a rabbi who was approached at the conclusion of the Sabbath Service by a young woman whom he had never seen before. "Rabbi," she said, "I'm going to kill myself. I am a worthless person. My mother and I lived together. We had only each other. Yet we quarreled all the time. Many times I said, 'I wish you would drop dead!' Well, I got my wish. She died two weeks ago. Now I'm all alone and I don't want to live any more." When he had regained his composure, the rabbi said to her: "Come back to my study on Monday. In the meantime I will try to find a psychiatrist for you and he will take care of you." The woman turned away silently, walked out of the synagogue, and did not return. It is obvious that the rabbi was too shocked to fulfill his role properly.

Perhaps the rabbi felt that a person who threatens suicide hardly ever commits it. Let us banish for all time the old bromide that suicidal attempts and gestures are not really to be taken seriously. No threat may be minimized. Even if the person is indulging in dramatics to gain attention, he needs to be watched carefully and helped.

How might the rabbi have proceeded in the above situation? He should not have allowed the woman to leave the synagogue with what might have seemed to her an abrupt dismissal. If he were unable to see her at that moment, he immediately should have made an appointment to see her later that day. To demonstrate his genuine interest and concern for her welfare, he could have given her his telephone number and in turn taken hers. He could have ascertained where she lived as well as the names of her close friends to be recruited for supportive help.

Ironically enough, many still regard people who attempt suicide, and survive, as failures. Thus they earn the double opprobrium of being considered so deranged that they wanted to die and so incompetent that they could not do the job properly. The clergyman should never underestimate the immediate help he might render. The rabbi in his symbolic role influences the behavior of even a violently irrational person. He is in the position to exercise authority as a religious counselor and parent substitute. The pastor's powers are often judged to be almost as those of the "Father in Heaven." As the exponent of the external mysteries of God, he might help the individual to be guided through the pains and hurts of life. He works not with mechanical tools but with spiritual instruments that operate in the cure of souls.

The first step in establishing rapport with the troubled person is through the techniques of responsive listening, catharsis, and acceptance. Instead of chastisement, the person should be put at ease. The clergyman might say, "The fact that you wanted to see me or speak about what is troubling you is commendable. For all of us have our limits of endurance. It takes strength to seek help. To consider suicide is an attempt to solve overwhelming problems. By coming here, you demonstrate that you are seeking a better solution. Let's talk together."

There are no cut and dried answers to the recondite problem of suicide. But the rabbi can initially assist by demonstrating an unshakable attitude of acceptance towards the troubled person. Much depends on this quality of relationship. It should be one not only of words but a non-verbal communication of empathy; not the moment of pontifical moralizing, but of loving support and understanding. The clergyman should stay close to the potential suicide's ego and not be detached.

The goal of any approach should be to minimize feelings

of guilt and fear of rejection. A message of hope and help should be communicated. Once a transference has been established, the counselee may be given greater insight into the precise nature and reality of his self-destructiveness to the end that tension and discomfort be decreased and mitigated. The clinical treatment might be effected by the therapist, but courage and support are offered by the religious leader. Perhaps when the person's life situation is re-examined, satisfactory solutions may be offered with new strengths and new alternatives. The problem could stem from reality factors which the person had never taken into consideration. Or there could be consequences which he had failed to anticipate, memories which had long been repressed, or aggressions which he had heretofore never recognized. Attention should also be directed to the relatives and family so that they may be helped to accept the suicidal attempt as well as the patient's limitations. Environmental changes are often essential for the counselee's future health and security. Constructive planning is discussed with the person. Suicidal tendencies remain most acute until desirable alterations in the life ensue. Follow up—such as environmental manipulation and psychotherapy—is helpful so that the aggressiveness is displaced with the challenge of growth.

The religious leader can assist greatly in the post-treatment phase. The individual is encouraged to take an active role in the fellowship of the religious community. Still, the clergyman cannot relax. Once the crisis is past, improvement is often confused with the patient's increase of psychomotor energy. Just prior to suicide, many depressed people rush into a welter of activity and contritely apologize to anyone whom they think they have offended. Thus, we are often misled into thinking the worst is over; we breathe a sigh of relief and let our guard down. But the worst is yet to come, for this phase often reflects only an inner resolve to mend things by doing away with themselves. And indeed, half the individuals do commit suicide within 90 days after the emotional crisis.

The clergyman should also remember that he is not alone.

The greatest progress in the field of suicide has been attained by a "suicide squad" in which the minister is a vital cog. What foresight was evidenced in England when in 1774 a Royal Humane Society was formed with a team devoted to frustrate attempted suicides! Today there are a number of agencies for the prevention of suicide: *National Save-A-Life League* in New York; *Rescue, Incorporated,* in Boston and Worcester; *Anti-Suicide Department* of the Salvation Army in London. In Boston with *Rescue, Incorporated,* out of a total of 1,000 cases recorded (there is a 24 hour telephone service which can bring help to a person on the brink of ending his life), only one completed suicide occurred. What has added to its effectiveness is that the head of the staff, Rev. Kenneth B. Murphy, does not work unilaterally. The agency is significantly located at the Boston City Hospital and boasts a staff of 70 members including rabbis, ministers, priests, physicians, psychologists, psychiatrists, and social workers.

Is the clergyman able by himself to undergo the emotional strain during the suicidal crisis? A team can share this grave responsibility. Is the minister knowledgeable in the depth meanings of suicide? Other experts have been given specialized training in this area. Will the counselee take his own life and should he be hospitalized? A trained therapist could more accurately decide the wisdom of such treatment and the advantages of an institution especially if there are the attendant indications of schizophrenia, alcoholism, and impulsive psychopathic tendencies. Admittedly, referral is a delicate matter and should be handled so that the anxious person need not construe it as a cold, peremptory dismissal. But if action is deferred too long, the threat may become a reality. There are various agencies and community resources which should be tapped to bring about the most effectual handling of the presuicidal person. The data of these agencies is of inestimable assistance in detection and aid to others as well.

The rabbi is never freed from his responsibility to the potential suicide. He becomes a part—an important part—of the total treatment. *Ex officio,* as a priest, he contributes his own special orientation based upon a religious faith, but as pastor, he represents a friend and member of the family. His role is not confined to crises. He is there in normal times of prosperity and happiness.

Karl Menninger mentions in the treatment of potential suicidal persons the need for a love object to replace that which had been lost through death or abandonment. The religious leader, with the aid of his sensitive members, could simulate a loving family atmosphere and assist the disquieted person to feel that there is a religious fellowship in the community bound together by ties of sympathy, love, and mutual concern. Like the mission sign for the alcoholic and the abandoned, the synagogue could be: "A Friend to the Friendless." Ritual and prayer could enhance the suggestibility that the troubled person truly belongs in the ever-embracing religious relationship. And a concept of a loving God is extremely helpful. In Gordon Allport's words (*The Individual and His Religion*): "To many people a sense of cosmic affiliation is needed to round out and to order the sum total of their attachments. Love of God is needed in order to make life seem complete and intelligible and right."

Religion establishes a power of faith. A search for meaning in one's existence is one of man's most primary concerns. Helping him to believe in God may give him the courage and fortitude to change his life and attitudes. Through a religious orientation, the rabbi alleviates some of the fears that induced the suicidal tendency. By posing spiritual alternatives to the counselee's ultimate anxieties, i.e., death, guilt, suffering, failure, he communicates to the suicidal person a meaningful purposefulness of life.

Especially might the clergyman be helpful in relieving feelings of guilt. He aids by modifying an overstrict conscience and softening it to permit the individual a more normal or bearable range of human living. Mortimer Ostow and Ben Ami Scharfstein devote the preponderance of their book, *The Need to Believe,* to the effective religious methods and mechanisms for dissipating guilt through reparation, confession, ritual, repentance, and atonement. The pastor, acting in a symbolic role for the God of forgiveness, may greatly assist in relieving the feelings of that troubled and tormented soul.

The rabbi plays a significant role in the treatment of the potential suicidal person through pastoral counseling—in extending his loving concern, in imparting a religious orientation of life, a feeling of belonging, a power of faith, and a meaningful belief in God. By being able to recognize the symptoms of a possible suicidal person, by referring the individual to the proper agencies, and by helping in the post-treatment phase within the fellowship of a religious community, he is of boundless value and help. Not to be overlooked is his participation in community programs to overcome the popular prejudices and misinformation regarding the entire area of suicide. He should submit his own findings to child guidance clinics, judges, policemen, physicians, and others in a position to help recognize and understand the pre-suicidal person. Case histories with vital data regarding those members who have either attempted or committed suicide would be invaluable in bringing further light to bear in this thorny field of darkness and ignorance. The religious leader would be participating not only in supportive therapy but in preventative therapy as well. He would then be truly worthy of the Hebrew designation spoken in the Twenty Third Psalm: *Roeh,* "a shepherd to his people."

VI. *Counseling the Family of the Suicide*

"Death remains the one citadel of mystery which autonomous man is compelled to surrender to God." So said Theodore O. Wedel in his *Christianity of Main Street.* In the case of suicide, however, the platitude cannot be uttered that the only uncertain thing about death is the time it will occur.

The Jewish writer Ibn Pakuda Bahya calls the suicide "a sentinel who deserted his post." Suicide is often called self-murder, the infraction of the Sixth Commandment. And so Menander, in his *Monostikoi,* put it: "Not death is dreadful but a shameful death." The affirmation in many religious traditions is that the self-murderer is to be held in scorn, derision, and contempt with denial of proper burial rites and right of interment in holy ground. "The act of suicide is a crime," many say piously, "the worst crime of all."

If death is a traumatic experience for the survivors, *a fortiori,* how much more so is the self-willed and self-executed death of a loved one. What intolerable feelings of guilt and grief are aroused! How difficult to face one's neighbors and one's friends! What a feeling of utter rejection! The "unpardonable sin" has been performed; the universal taboo with its theological imprimatur has been ignominiously violated. It is in this context that the clergyman is often called.

The goals in ministering to the family of the suicide are similar to those in helping all members face bereavement. In Erich Lindemann's words: "Grief work is emancipation from the bondage to the deceased, readjustment to the environment in which the deceased is missing, and the formation of new relationships." Yet where suicide is involved the problem becomes more involved. The religious leader, himself, may have guilt feelings for not having detected the symptoms. Or if he had previously seen that member in a counseling situation, he may now feel that he was a complete and utter failure for not having succeeded in warding off the tragedy.

The rabbi should understand that the degree of his acceptability to the bereaved will in a large measure depend upon his previous relationship to them. If he had not been close to the family or if the mourners feel that he may be judicative toward them because of the suicide, then the religious leader may have difficulty in establishing rapport with members of the family. Even if there has been a good relationship in the past, the people may withdraw because of their own guilt feelings or projection of recrimination upon the clergyman because as the Father-God surrogate, he, "God's Priest," allowed this to happen.

The rabbi does not ascertain the emotional state of the bereaved through cross-questioning but rather through empathy and understanding. The spirit of caring and compassion communicates itself to the bereaved. But not always on the first visit. Very often the most effective counseling comes after the funeral service. Before the ceremony itself, there may be incredulous disbelief and the needed expenditure of time for the physical arrangements of the burial.

The funeral itself offers an opportunity to comfort the mourners. It is the rite of separation. The "bad dream" is real. The presence of the corpse actualizes the experience. The process of denial is gradually transformed to the acceptance of reality.

In the eulogy, the clergyman should avoid any reference to blasphemy. Certainly the positive aspects of the life should be mentioned. The rabbi could also accentuate the thought that the mysteries of life and death are too vast for the human mind to comprehend. We put our trust in God. The loved one is with Him—the "Lord of Life and Death." After the service, the outstretched arms of friends demonstrate acceptance and sustaining affection.

When the funeral is over, the religious leader has the task of reconciling the bereaved to his loss. In the process, he should pay particular attention to possible grief reactions which could lead to personal disintegration and mental illness. According to Louis Linn, "Among the factors that may precipitate a distorted mourning reaction is an untimely loss. A death for which one is completely unprepared will usually have a more devastating impact than death from a chronic disease." When the grief work is not done, the person may suffer morbid grief characterized by delayed and distorted reactions. He may show great fortitude at the funeral but later develop symptoms of somatic disease or agitated depression. This may include the actual denial of the death with schizophrenic tendencies or psychosomatic disease such as hypochondriasis, ulcerative colitis, rheumatoid arthritis, and asthma. Obsessive-compulsive behavior may manifest itself where the bereaved appeases his guilt through extreme cleanliness. Or an unwillingness to terminate the effects of the funeral service, i.e., "Tell me the eulogy again." There may be self-punitive behavior detrimental to his social and economic existence. It must be noted that the line of demarcation between "normal psychological aspects of bereavement" and "distorted mourning reactions" is thin indeed, just as is the hiatus between "normality" and "neurosis." Each symptom must be viewed not as a single and decisive entity but in the framework of the total composition and of the schematic formulations.

In comforting the bereaved, thought must be given to the *special kind* of death. The rabbi starts by accepting the survivors. In addition he may enlist the support of selected congregants who demonstrate that their love is not diminished because of the act of suicide. The interest should be genuine and in the propriety of good taste. Over-indulgence engenders further guilt reactions.

The family may still feel guilty and very much to blame. The guilt may take the form of self-recrimination, depression, and hostility. A tendency is to look for a scapegoat, often one who is least able to bear the added burden. There may be a direct charge: "You killed him! You allowed it to happen!" Inwardly the indictor may accuse himself but turns the anger outward in the attempt to cope with his own guilt. Minor omissions come to mind and loom as major, significant causes of death. Again and again, he replays the ninth inning by devising those plays that might have won the game and preserved the life.

In this area, the clergyman can be extremely effective. The helplessness that assails the grief-stricken often leads them to envisage the role of the religious leader in a symbolic aspect, as the representative of God. As such, he can assuage intense feelings of guilt by offering a meaningful concept of forgiveness and absolution to the family of the suicide, as well as help them transform the errors of the past into a loving memorial by more noble living in the future.

In the attempt to fight off repugnant thoughts about the deceased's self-imposed death, the mourner often becomes obsessed with the latter's good qualities. The loved one becomes a model, an exemplar. This idealization and retrospective falsification is out of proportion to the actuality. In the identification with the lost person, there exists the danger of copying the symptoms of the last act of death. The surviving member believes that he, too, possesses similar characteristics to the deceased. His own judgment is constantly called to question. Self-eradication may seem the only proper way out. The symptoms of the deceased suicide become transferred to the bereaved. The survivor may think: "I've got to kill myself. My father did it and I am just like him. I feel like I am losing my mind."

Since suicide is a blow and an affront to humanity, we repeatedly try to defend ourselves by saying that the suicide was out of his mind. But to tell a grieving person that his loved one was "crazy" does not lighten the burden. Nor is it the truth. To quote Schneidman, Farberow, and Litman: "The majority of persons who commit suicide are tormented and ambivalent; they may be neurotic or have a character disorder, but *they are not insane*." Telling the survivors that the person was crazy does not add to their social status, but brings only the fear of inherited mental disease. The clergyman might say: "There is much we do not know about suicide but we do know there is a limit to the load any person can bear. At that moment, death appeared the only alternative to a troubled life. Just as in Maimonides' words, 'God's ways are not our ways,' so are the ways of those closest to us not necessarily our own ways." The religious leader can give an assurance which is predicated upon empirical studies: "This I can tell you: suicide is not inherited."

Especially in a case of suicide the bereaved wishes to pour out his heart. The religious leader encourages grief work by responsive listening and empathetic discernment. Sigmund Freud mentioned the "ties of dissolution"—that is, reviewing with the bereaved every experience with the dead person. As each experience is reviewed, a pang of pain is felt at the thought that the experience will never be repeated. As the pang is experienced, the bereaved is able to dissolve himself of his emotional ties with the person no longer alive and thus establish new relationships by which the mourner may take an active place in the company of the living. Comfort is given even as the bereaved is challenged to renewed growth.

Religion may help the family face grief by furnishing them

with an intimation of immortality. How reassuring it would be if the religious leader, within the individual theological framework, can say: "I do not believe that your loved one is consigned to hell and damnation. God's love is eternal. You can trust Him." The pastor might also aid the mourner with a concept of life-after-death consistent with his religious faith.

The Psalmist wisely spoke of "walking through the valley of the shadow of death." Sometimes one forgets that the valley is open on both sides. Having entered it, we need not make of it a permanent dwelling place. After we have lingered there a while, we can walk through it and out. With the same Psalmist, we may yet affirm: "Though weeping tarries in the night, joy may come in the morning."

The religious leader's primary objective is to aid in the emergence of a new self which has assimilated the grief experience and grown because of and through it. With the aid and encouragement of a clergyman who is kind, sympathetic, and understanding, the bereaved may be helped to accept the horrible death through a more profound and meaningful religious approach to life. By the rabbi's evaluation of the experience, by catharsis, confession, remembrance, and release, the members are guided to new purposes. Their introspection may bring new value judgments of life and love and meaning. Even the house of worship will no longer be an impersonal entity, since the members have extended their hands in warmth and affection. But most important is the comfort they will gain from a new and abiding concept of God: "Even though I cry in the bereavement of my heart when my beloved is taken from this earth, may it be as a child cries who knows his father is near and who clings unafraid to a trusted hand. In this spirit, O Thou Who art the Master of My Destiny, do I commit that which is so precious into Thy keeping."

Epilogue

Life and death come into the world together; the eyes and the sockets which hold them are created at the same moment. From the moment I am born I am old enough to die. Life and death are contained within each other, complete each other and are understandable in terms of each other. *How* to die means nothing less than *how* to live.

Going into the question of suicide means breaking open taboos. Suicide puts society and religion, and the community of souls *in extremis*. Self-destruction is the paradigm of the individual's independence from everyone else. This is the reason the law labels it criminal and religion has called it sin.

Religious, sociological and psychological views aid the clergyman to understand some of the root metaphors which govern the person's attitudes and loyalties. But the religious leader must first begin with that person, not with the concept. In D. H. Laurence's *Healing*: "I am not a mechanism, an assembly of various sections. I am ill because of wounds to soul, to the deep emotional self." The rabbi is devoted to the treatment of the "wounds of the soul." He must accept creative tension which does not run away from crises. By his love and support to those who cry for help, may it be said of him: "He who saves one soul is imputed by God as if he saves the entire world."

Bibliography

Allport, Gordon W. *The Individual and His Religion*. New York: The Macmillan Company, 1960.

Argyle, Michael. *Religious Behavior*. Glencoe, Illinois: Free Press, 1959.

The Babylonian Talmud. Berakoth, 23a, Seder Zeraim, Volume I. London: The Soncino Press, 1948.

The Babylonian Talmud. Hullin, 94a, Seder Kodashim, Volume IV. London: The Soncino Press, 1948.

Batchelor, I. R. C. *Alcoholism and Attempted Suicide*. Journal of Mental Science, Number 419, April 1954.

Caro, Joseph. *Code of Jewish Law*. Translated by Hyman Goldin. New York: Hebrew Publishing Company, 1927.

Dublin, Louis I. *Suicide: A Sociological and Statistical Study*. New York: The Ronald Press, 1963.

Dublin, Louis I. and Bunzel, Bessie. *To Be or Not To Be.* New York: Harrison Smith and Robert Haas, 1933.

Durkheim, Emile. *Suicide, A Study in Sociology.* Glencoe, Illinois: Free Press, 1951.

Ellis, E. R. and Allen, G. N. *Within Our Suicide Problem.* New York: Doubleday and Company, Inc., 1961.

Farberow, Norman L. and Schneidman, Edwin S. *The Cry For Help.* New York: McGraw-Hill Book Company, Inc., 1961.

Fenichel, Otto. *The Psychoanalytic Theory of Neurosis.* New York: W. W. Norton and Company, 1945.

Freehof, Solomon B. *Reform Jewish Practice and Its Rabbinic Background.* New York: Hebrew Union College Press, 1960.

Freud, Sigmund. *Mourning and Melancholia.* Collected Papers, Volume IV. London: Hogarth Press, Ltd., 1925.

Hadas, Moses. *The Third and Fourth Books of Maccabees.* New York: Harper and Brothers, 1953.

Harada, Tasuku. *Suicide, Japanese.* Encyclopedia of Religion and Ethics, Volume XII. New York: Charles Scribner's Sons, 1955.

Harper, Robert A. *Psychoanalysis and Psychotherapy.* New Jersey: Prentice-Hall, Inc., 1959.

Henderson, D. K. and Gillespie, A. *A Text Book of Psychiatry for Students and Practitioners.* London: Oxford University Press, 1927.

Hendin, Herbert M. *What the Pastor Ought to Know About Suicide.* Pastoral Psychology, Volume IV, Number 39, December 1953.

Henry, Andrew F. and Short, James F. *Suicide and Homicide.* Glencoe, Illinois: Free Press, 1954.

Hillman, James. *Suicide and The Soul.* New York and Evanston: Harper and Row Publishers, 1964.

Hiltner, Seward. *Suicidal Reflections.* Pastoral Psychology, Volume IV, Number 39, December 1953, pp. 33–45.

Holy Scriptures, According to the Masoretic Text. Philadelphia: Jewish Publication Society of America, 1951.

Ives, Hendrick. *Facts and Theories of Psychoanalysis*. New York: Alfred A. Knopf, 1948.

Johnson, Paul E. *Psychology of Pastoral Care*. New York and Nashville: Abingdon Press, 1953.

Jung, Carl. *Modern Man in Search of a Soul*. New York: Harcourt, Brace and Company, 1933.

Kessel, Neil. *Death By Choice*. Abbottempo, Volume III, Number 2, May 12, 1965, p. 2.

Lawson, Herbert G. *Focus on Suicide*. The Wall Street Journal, Volume CLXII, Number 58, p. 1.

Liebman, Joshua L. *Peace of Mind*. New York: Simon and Schuster, Inc., 1946.

Lindemann, Eric and Greer, Ina M. *A Study of Grief: Emotional Responses to Suicide*. Pastoral Psychology, Volume IV, Number 39, December 1953, pp. 10–13.

Linn, Louis and Schwarz, Leo W. *Psychiatry and Religious Experience*. New York: Random House, 1958.

Loomis, Earl. *Pastoral Psychology*, Volume IV, Number 39, December 1953, pp. 52–53.

Malev, Milton. *The Value of Ritual*. Judaism and Psychiatry. New York: The National Academy for Adult Jewish Studies, 1956.

Man On A Ledge. Rescue, Inc., 115 Southampton Street, Boston, Mass.

Marti-Ibanez. *On Christmas and Neuroses*. MD Publications, Number 111. New York.

Meerloo, Joost A. M. *Suicide and Mass Suicide*. New York: Grune and Stratton, Inc.

Menninger, Karl. *Man Against Himself*. New York: Harcourt, Brace and Company, Inc., 1938.

Moss, Leonard and Hamilton, D. G. *Psychotherapy of the Suicidal Patient*. American Journal of Psychiatry, 1956, pp. 814–820.

Murphy, Rev. Kenneth B., Order of St. John of God. *The Flame, A Quarterly*. The Brothers of the Hospitaller.

Oates, Wayne E. *The Funeral of A Suicide*. Pastoral Psychology, Volume IV, Number 39, December 1953, pp. 14–17.

Ostow, Mortimer and Scharfstein, Ben Ami. *The Need to*

Believe. New York: International Universities Press, Inc., 1954.

Reines, Ch. W. *The Jewish Attitude Toward Suicide*. Judaism, Volume X, Number 2, Spring 1961, pp. 160–170.

Revel, Hirschel. *Suicide*. The Universal Jewish Encyclopedia, Volume X. New York: Universal Jewish Encyclopedia Company, 1948.

Reznikoff, Charles. *Flavius Josephus*. Universal Jewish Encyclopedia, Volume VI. New York: Universal Jewish Encyclopedia Company, 1942.

Sainsbury, Peter. *Suicide in London, An Ecological Study*. London: Basic Books, Inc., 1955.

Shearer, Lloyd. *Can Suicide Be Prevented?* Parade, March 3, 1963.

Schneidman, Edwin S. and Farberow, Norman. *Clues To Suicide*. New York: McGraw-Hill Book Company, 1957.

Schrut, Albert. *Suicidal Adolescents and Children*. Journal of the American Medical Association, Volume CLXXXVIII, June 29, 1964, pp. 1103–1107.

Shilleto, A. R. *Flavius Josephus, Antiquities of the Jews*. Book VI, Volume I. London: George Bell and Sons, 1900.

Shilleto, A. R. *Flavius Josephus, The Jewish Wars*. Book II, Volume V. London: George Bell and Sons, 1903.

Shilleto, A. R. *Flavius Josephus, The Jewish Wars*. Book III, Volume IV. London: George Bell and Sons, 1903.

Solomon, Philip. *When You Must Act to Block Suicide*. Consultant, November 1963.

Southard, Samuel. *The Minister's Role in Attempted Suicide*. Pastoral Psychology, Volume IV, Number 39, December 1953, pp. 27–32.

Sprott, S. E. *The English Debate on Suicide*. LaSalle, Illinois: Open Court Publishing Company, 1961.

Stengel, E. and Cook, Nancy G. *Attempted Suicide, Its Social Significance and Effects*. London: Chapman and Hall, Ltd., 1958.

Suicide. Encyclopedia of Religion and Ethics, Volume III. New York: Charles Scribner's Sons, 1955.

Suicide. Jewish Encyclopedia, Volume XI. New York: Funk and Wagnalls Company, 1905.

Whalen, Elsa. *Religion and Suicide.* Review of Religious Research, Winter 1964.

Williams, Glanville L. *The Sanctity of Life and The Criminal Law.* New York: Alfred A. Knopf, 1948.

Yessler, Paul G. and Becker, Herman A. *On the Communication of Suicidal Ideas.* Archives of General Psychiatry, Volume V, December 1960.

Zeitlin, Solomon. *The Second Book of Maccabees.* New York: Harper and Brothers, 1954.